HIGH LEVEL ROUTE
CHAMONIX-ZERMATT-SAAS

Dana Coffield

HIGH LEVEL ROUTE
Chamonix · Zermatt · Saas

Ski mountaineering in the Mont Blanc Range and
Pennine Alps

WITH SUMMER ROUTE SUPPLEMENT

ERIC ROBERTS

WEST COL PRODUCTIONS

First published in Great Britain 1973 by
West Col Productions
Goring   Reading   Berks.   RG8   9AA

Reprinted 1978
Second Edition 1984

SBN   906227   25   9

High Level Route
Eric Bernard Roberts (1945-1979)

Printed in England by
Swindon Press Ltd   Swindon   Wilts.

CONTENTS

LIST OF ILLUSTRATIONS

DIAGRAMS

PLATES

grouped between pages 64-65

Cover: Eric Roberts skiing near the Petit Combin in 1965, showing a Swiss postage stamp depicting the Matterhorn issued in that year and used by the author to write home.

Frontis: Eric Roberts descending from the Col de l'Evêque towards the upper basin of the Haut Arolla glacier, 1967.

Opposite: Eric Roberts' party resting on the Otemma glacier, looking back to Mont Gelé.

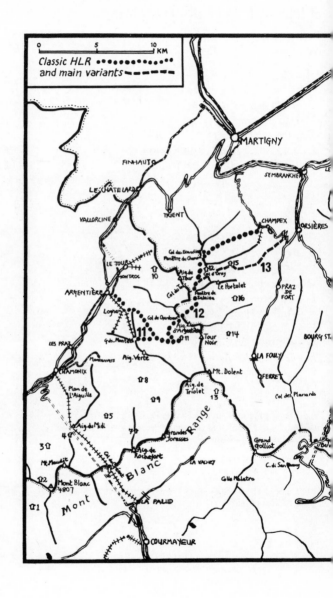

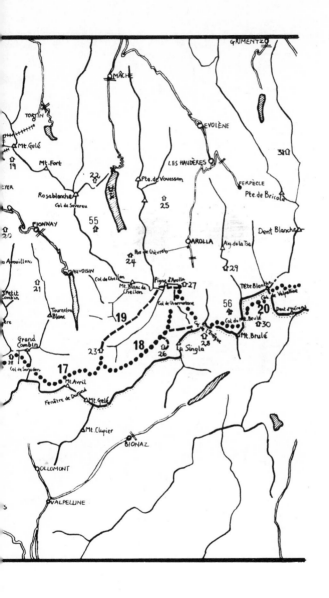

⌂ HUTS

1. Gonella
2. Vallot
3. Grands Mulets
4. Col du Midi Lab.
5. Requin
6. Torino
7. Périades biv.
8. Couvercle
9. Leschaux
10. Albert Premier
11. Argentière
12. Trient
13. Fiorio biv.
14. A Neuve
15. Orny
16. Saleina
17. Vélan
18. Valsorey
19. Mont Fort
20. Brunet
21. Panossière
22. Prafleuri
23. Chanrion
24. Dix
25. Aigs. Rouges
26. Singla biv.
27. Vignettes
28. Principessa di Piemonte
29. Bertol
30. Aosta
31. Moiry
32. Schönbiel
33. Mountet
34. Tracuit
35. Turtmann
36. Rothorn
37. Theodul
38. Mezzalama
39. Cesare e Giorgio biv.
40. Quintino Sella
41. Gnifetti
42. Balmenhorn biv.
43. Margherita
44. Gallarate biv.
45. Monte Rosa
46. Fluhalp inn
47. Täsch
48. Dom
49. Bordier
50. Längfluh inn
51. Britannia
52. Weissmies
53. Almagelleralp inn
54. Malnate
55. Pantalons
56. Bouquetins
57. Almagell

ABBREVIATIONS

Aig.	Aiguille
approx.	approximately
c.	circa (approximately)
CAF	Club Alpin Français
CAI	Club Alpino Italiano
E	east
HLR	High Level Route
h.	hour(s)
km.	kilometre(s)
LK	Landeskarte der Schweiz (Swiss federal map)
L	left
m.	metre(s)
min.	minutes
mtn(s).	mountain(s)
N	north
p.	page (reference)
pt.	point (map reference, spot height)
R	right
SAC	Schweizer Alpen-Club
S	south
trig.	trigonometrical
W	west

Other directions appearing in this guidebook, e.g. NE, SW (north-east, south-west), etc. will be taken as read.

PART I

GENERAL INFORMATION

INTRODUCTION

The High Level Route traverses eleven glacier passes amongst the great Alpine peaks from Chamonix in the west to Saas Fee in the east. As the most famous and highly prized ski tour in the Alps, and for that matter in the world, it holds a unique attraction for ski mountaineers and tourers as well as for a surprisingly large percentage of piste skiers. This fact probably accounts for considerable discrepancies in reports regarding the technical nature of the undertaking. Contrary to popular belief in climbing circles, given reasonable conditions there are no particular problems to trouble a competent mountaineer who skis steadily. On the other hand the piste skier, unused to the physical demands of an ascent and unaware of general mountaineering hazards, has a different concept of difficulties and can come unstuck.

The classic High Level Route (HLR), the finest line practical on ski, covers an effective distance of about 130 km. It is normally divided into nine stages. Logical breaks at valley resorts occur twice. It starts at Argentière, about 8 km. up the valley from Chamonix, with the soft option of a cableway ride, and crosses the northern part of the Mont Blanc Range from France into Switzerland to reach Champex at the end of the first self-contained section. Here the gap on the HLR between the Val Ferret and Val d'Entremont is bridged by a road journey to Bourg St. Pierre below the Great St. Bernard pass. The main section of the tour leads across the south shoulder of the Grand Combin to the deserted heart of the Western Pennine Alps at the head of the Val de Bagnes. It continues near the backbone of the range on the Swiss side of the frontier ridge, apart from a sole short passage on Italian terrain before the magnificent

13

descent below the Matterhorn to Zermatt. Finally the route passes the foot of the Monte Rosa on the roundabout way to the Adlerpass and Saas Fee. Ascents and descents combined total almost 20,000 metres. The route runs at an average altitude of 3000m. and paradoxically the lowest pass crossed, the Fenêtre du Chamois (2985m.), is usually the most awkward. These qualities of length, height, its sustained nature and the continuity of an aesthetically pleasing line, combined with splendid surroundings, explain the unparalleled reputation of this ski tour.

Numerous variations to the HLR are frequently preferred to the classic itinerary. Several of these alternatives pursue equally or more elegant lines, notably the traverse of the Pigne d'Arolla. However, any route that evades the hardest stage across the Grand Combin zone remains unsatisfactory from the mountaineering point of view. Guides, who understandably do not want the responsibility of negotiating this key passage with uncertain tourists, commonly set out from Verbier and traverse the Rosablanche group to join the classic route later at the Vignettes hut above Arolla.

In recent years new cableways have been responsible for additional variations; indeed, if all the existing projects should materialize, then a largely downhill HLR would become possible. Sadly, little voluntary restraint has been shown in the commercial exploitation of the high mountains. More encouragingly, present Swiss government policy temporarily prohibits the realization of major uphill transport projects affecting glaciated regions.

In the broadest sense of the term the HLR comprises all traverses that link Chamonix, Argentière, Le Tour, Courmayeur, Bourg St. Pierre and Verbier in the west with Zermatt, Saas Fee, Saas Almagell, Cervinia, Gressoney, Alagna and Macugnaga in the east. Certain valleys that rise to the south from the Rhone valley, in particular the Val de Bagnes and Val d'Hérens (Arolla), connect at their head with the HLR.

The skier who does not really appreciate the mountains and who judges a tour by the quality of the skiing only will probably be disappointed by the HLR. While some magnificent ski descents should be experienced, difficult snow conditions sometimes mar a downhill run for the tourer and the necessity of skiing conservatively in remote surroundings with a heavy rucksack acts as a restricting influence. Skis are to a certain extent the means to an end. Other criteria also motivate the tourer: a spirit of adventure, pleasure and a sense of achievement derived from moving amidst changing scenery, the contrast between high passes and the valleys, the solitude of the mountains. For the piste basher, touring opens up a new horizon free from lift queues, overcrowded pistes and repetitive runs. Approached with the right attitude and without false preconceptions the HLR gives a memorable experience amidst unforgettable surroundings.

The original concept of this guidebook to the HLR has been considerably expanded by a comprehensive survey of ski mountaineering in the Mont Blanc Range and Pennine Alps (Part V). But difficult winter climbs are not considered. Many ski tourers wish to combine hut to hut traverses with ascents of the major ski peaks. Nevertheless, parties who cannot resist the great temptation to prolong the HLR by climbing mountains on the way should remember that each day spent thus reduces the chances of finishing the tour before the weather breaks. On the main section of the tour from Bourg St. Pierre to Zermatt, even without such additions, the weather sometimes makes it necessary to replenish food supplies in Arolla. Individuals must decide where their priorities lie. Peaks commonly ascended by minor detours off the HLR are noted in the text. Some huts that serve as a base for a broad selection of outstanding mountains on ski are well worth visiting in their own right, perhaps after completing the HLR or by returning another year. Foremost in this category come the Panossière (Grand Combin group), Monte Rosa and Britannia huts.

In an average season April and May produce the most favourable conditions for the HLR. Ski tours are rarely undertaken in glaciated regions before March. Despite the fact that ski mountaineers pioneered the HLR in January and February at the beginning of the century, winter is now recognized as the least suitable period: unconsolidated snow deceptively conceals crevasses, powder snow avalanches are hard to predict, the wind sweeps light snow off steep slopes leaving bare ice in places, no huts are wardened and above all the intense cold combined with

15

short days exaggerates any problems. However, while glacier skiing improves as spring advances, simultaneously the snow cover in the valleys melts and these two factors must be counterbalanced. Ideal conditions for ski ascents of Mont Blanc and in the Monte Rosa-Breithorn group still occur in June.

HISTORY

Although most of the passes on the HLR had already been crossed or visited, it was not until 1860 that a concerted effort was made to link them by a continuous traverse. At that time this was a tougher proposition due to the absence of alpine club huts. The route was virtually completed by members of the Alpine Club in 1861, though an ideal line between the N part of the Mont Blanc Range and the Pennine Alps was not found until the following summer. The explorations of several parties contributed to the original HLR. J. F. Hardy, F. W. Jacomb, W. Mathews, F. F. Tuckett and S. Winkworth were the principal driving forces behind these expeditions, while forerunners such as J. D. Forbes and A. Wills had played an important role. Their guides included J. B. and M. Croz, A. Simond, P. Perren and G. Kronig. The route opened in 1861 led from Chamonix across the Col d'Argentière to La Fouly and via Orsières to Bourg St. Pierre. (The traverse of the Col des Planards was first made in 1862.) It then went via the Col de Sonadon and Col d'Oren to Prarayé, and finally across the Col de Valpelline to Zermatt. They named their route the High Level Road: consequently the term "Haute Route", the later French translation of the name that has been adopted by all nationalities in their apparent ignorance of the history of the Golden Age of Alpine climbing, is a misnomer for a British invention.

Of course, the HLR was pioneered as a summer expedition on foot, for skis were only introduced to the Alps towards the end of the 19th century. With no mechanized uphill transport available in that era, not surprisingly it was winter climbers who soon experimented with skis. Outstanding early ski ascents included the Dufourspitze in 1898, the Breithorn in 1899, the Strahlhorn in 1901, Mont Vélan and the Cima di Jazzi in 1902.

In January 1903 J. Couttet, M. Payot, J. Ravanel and A. Simond attempted the first ski traverse of the HLR. In winter conditions and on ski the summer version required certain modifications. This party crossed the Col du Chardonnet and the Fenêtre de Saleina to Orsières and then reached the Chanrion hut by the Val de Bagnes, thereby completely avoiding the Grand Combin massif. Near the Col de l'Evêque bad weather forced a retreat and the tour was abandoned. The Vignettes hut had not then been built. However, they travelled round by road to Les Haudères and continued across the Col d'Hérens to Zermatt.

In February 1903, just one month later, R. Helbling and F. Reichert with A. Pellaud made a remarkable ski traverse of the Pennine Alps from the Val de Bagnes to Zermatt. They ascended to the Panossière hut and crossed the N side of the Grand Combin massif near the Tournelon Blanc, experiencing a difficult and dangerous descent to the Chanrion hut by a route avoided nowadays; on the steepest section Pellaud lost his skis in preventing a personal slip and as a result returned alone to the valley. The other two continued unconventionally via the Col du Mont Rouge, Col de Cheilon and Col de Riedmatten to Arolla. They eventually reached Zermatt via the Bertol hut and the Col d'Hérens.

Some years passed without any improvements to the ski version of the HLR. Meanwhile the first ski ascents of Mont Blanc and the Grand Combin were achieved in 1904 and 1907 respectively. The Adlerpass, linking Zermatt and Saas Fee, was first crossed on ski in 1910. However, it only became common to continue the HLR to Saas Fee much later.

At last, in January 1911, M. Kurz and F. Roget with J. and M. Crettex, L. Murisier and L. Theytaz opened up the present-day classic route directly across the Western Pennines in the course of their journey from Bourg St. Pierre to Zermatt. From the Valsorey hut they climbed to the Plateau du Couloir, immediately S of the Grand Combin, then crossed the Col de Sonadon to the Chanrion hut. Further on this party took a roundabout way from the Col Collon via the Bertol hut in order to make the first winter ascent of the Dent Blanche.

In March 1926 M. Kurz, the most influential pioneer of ski mountaineering, and his companions found a new ski route into the heart of the Pennine Alps when they started at Verbier and crossed the Rosablanche group from the Mont Fort hut to the Dix hut. By continuing over the Pigne d'Arolla the link with the classic HLR was made.

For several decades the complete HLR on ski remained an exceptional expedition. The passage of the Plateau du Couloir was in fact not repeated until 1927. But during the post-war years its popularity increased rapidly, to such an extent that overcrowded huts have become the norm around Easter and Whitsun. None the less, although tracks sometimes cover the entire route during the ski touring season, even then a short blizzard suffices to wipe out all previous traces and re-creates natural conditions. Nowadays the popularity of most ski peaks relates to their proximity to the HLR. Remote summits, in this context, remain comparatively neglected.

N.B. I have been unable to trace the date of the first British ski traverse of the HLR, but it most probably took place in the 1930s. Although the British opened up the HLR and recorded an outstanding number of first ascents in the Alps, they showed little interest in early ski mountaineering developments (with the notable exception of Arnold Lunn and W. A. Moore). Reliable sources indicate that no guideless British party had completed the classic HLR on ski as late as the mid 1950s.

DIFFICULTIES AND DANGERS
These vary so much from day to day during the season and from year to year than an attempt to adopt the conventional overall adjectival grading system, used to express the seriousness of summer routes, would serve little practical purpose. Instead the introductory general comments that precede each description should be interpreted according to the prevailing conditions: they indicate likely or possible problems. Comments on

difficulties, as opposed to dangers, on mtns. and pass traverses are made with the average ski mountaineer/tourer in mind; this point must be remembered by experienced alpine climbers and piste skiers alike whose scale of values will differ greatly. In ski mountaineering and touring, the objective dangers, magnified by the winter environment, usually outweigh by far the technical difficulties involved and they are outlined briefly here. None the less technical requirements must be considered first.

IN CLIMBING TERMS, given ideal snow conditions, no stage on the HLR exceeds F+ in standard if the remoteness of the situation and other circumstances peculiar to mtn. travel in winter/spring are excluded. But such conditions seldom prevail and on the key passage (Plateau du Couloir) ice screws or pegs may be needed. It therefore follows that guideless parties should carry basic climbing equipment (referred to later) and be practised in its use. Summit ascents assume alpine mountaineering experience if any rock climbing or narrow ridges, etc. are involved; it may then be expected that the route is likely to be appreciably harder or at least far more strenuous than in summer. Nor does it follow that steep snow slopes are easier in spring than in summer, because gales may have swept them clear of the powder snow that typifies winter precipitation. On the other hand, complex glaciers generally become far simpler to negotiate in spring once the winter snowfalls have consolidated.

IN SKIING TERMS very basic techniques suffice, namely the ability to do reliable stem turns in deep snow and to side-slip or do kick turns on steep slopes. It should be remembered that skiing with a heavy rucksack in awkward snow conditions towards the end of a long tour cannot be compared with a prepared piste run. Indeed, many experienced piste skiers are unable to execute their skills on unprepared runs. On doubtful slopes in descent do not hesitate to use closely linked kick turns, a prerequisite for the art of climbing steeply uphill on ski with skins. Finally, the importance of skiing carefully at all times, irrespective of one's skills, is emphasized: a broken leg in a remote situation on the HLR could have very serious consequences, especially in deteriorating weather which rules out helicopter rescue, and would at best prove a costly experience.

PHYSICAL FITNESS, incorporating acclimatization, plays a larger role than in average summer mountaineering. Tracking uphill in deep crusty snow or carrying skis on a heavy rucksack up a steep slope taxes one's muscles to the limit. And the tourer who starts the final downhill run in a weak state is clearly most prone to an accident. On the HLR a sustained effort is required for more than a week. Obviously prior training, preferably including pre-ski exercises or practice on an artificial ski slope and long walks or runs in rough country (sometimes carrying a rucksack), is therefore vital for a safe and enjoyable tour as opposed to a gruelling endurance test.

Common sense should dictate against setting out alone on any ski tour. Apart from the normal mtn. hazards encountered, any skier can break a leg on the easiest terrain. Even a party of two is vulnerable in the event of an accident. Four people who move at roughly the same speed, both uphill and downhill, form the ideal unit for safety purposes and for tracking in fresh snow. Large groups inevitably result in slower progress.

AVALANCHES constitute the most serious objective danger. The risk is greater in deeply cut valleys, sometimes encountered on hut approaches, than higher up on open glaciers. The snow texture on N facing slopes differs from that on S facing ones, etc. The likelihood of an avalanche anywhere varies greatly according to the prevailing snow conditions. The most dangerous period follows a heavy snowfall or possibly a gale, and the risk rises rapidly with the temperature. The absolute importance of an early start (03.00-06.00 according to the month) should be apparent in this respect. One must always not only consider the ground passed over, but also the slopes above that might send down an avalanche. The wet avalanches that spring conditions produce are far more predictable than the powder ones in winter. Windslab is the least foreseeable type of avalanche in spring. If a suspect slope cannot be avoided, then cross it as high up as possible and preferably on foot because avalanches are frequently initiated by skis cutting a slope. In the worst event the victim wearing an avalanche cord has a better chance of being located. On suspect terrain keep a considerable distance between each member of the party, undo security straps so that skis can be released if an avalanche occurs and take hands out of ski stick loops. Potentially dangerous zones are indicated in the descriptions. Open slopes angled between 30° and 40° statistically avalanche most, but never assume that everywhere else is safe because of all other factors involved (incl. temperature, wind, length, direction, etc.): even a 15° slope can avalanche.

Sérac avalanches are totally unpredictable but barely affect the HLR; the most notorious instance of this danger occurs on the Grand Combin. Cornices build up during the winter months and ridges that are straightforward in summer consequently become distinctly delicate.

CREVASSES are grossly underestimated by most skiers. The risk varies greatly according to the pattern of snowfalls in any given season. In winter, snowfalls do not consolidate due to the constant low temperature and merely conceal crevasses deceptively, thereby creating an illusion of safety. Once the snow has settled in spring the experienced ski tourer recognizes unsafe areas. Glaciers become steadily easier and safer during the course of spring. Moreover, a fall into an invisible crevasse is far less likely on ski than on foot because one's weight is distributed more evenly. Skiing downhill the chance of breaking into a crevasse is further reduced by one's speed, but all the same a clumsy turn or fall on the site of a crevasse can have disastrous consequences. In practice very few parties rope up for downhill skiing on the HLR, and roped skiing without talent and teamwork will result in farce; nevertheless it should not theoretically be shirked in heavily crevassed zones or in poor visibility. In ascent the rope causes little more bother than in summer and neglect is irrational. A fall is best held in the side-slipping position. Remember that when ascending a glacier by diagonal zigzags (the most comfortable way on steepish terrain) an entire party may be moving almost parallel to the same crevasse. If prussik loops are worn, these should be placed round one's boots straightaway because a crevasse victim may find it impossible to get his feet into the loops due to his skis. The difficulty of carrying out standard methods of crevasse rescue in a sudden emergency is often insufficiently recognized, particularly by small parties.

THE WEATHER forms the principal determining factor on any expedition. Snowfall and poor visibility combined clearly create the most serious circumstances. The scarcity of obvious landmarks in a winter landscape hampers orientation in such conditions far more than in summer. First-class map and compass work is then essential. Do not rely on tracks which can be obliterated within minutes and may also lead in the wrong direction. Retreat is not always practical. If lost, prepare a bivouac site rather than wander hopefully but aimlessly (an igloo or cave provides the best protection). In winter and spring, even on a fine day, extreme cold can cause frostbite, and foot movement is restricted on ski. This hazard applies above all to the highest glacier massifs (Mont Blanc, Grand Combin, Monte Rosa).

Sound judgement of situations and conditions is learnt by experience. The ski tourer must always be prepared to forgo an expedition if the weather is obviously deteriorating or the snow seems dangerous.

Unqualified parties are sometimes deterred from hiring a guide by the expense involved; that more accidents do not occur is due to luck rather than sound judgement. Many British ski tourers sensibly first visit the Eastern Alps to gain experience before embarking on longer expeditions in the higher Western Alps. Skiers uncertain of their ability to tackle the HLR or other ascents safely, due to limited touring experience or a lack of the normal mountaineering skills, etc., should join one of the many tours organized each spring by the guides' bureaux at the main touring centres. Routes are adapted to the capacity of the participants, make maximum use of cableways and usually avoid the principal mountaineering problems. The employment of a guide leaves the skier free to enjoy the downhill runs without any personal responsibilities for route finding, etc. On the other hand, such problems often represent an important element of the enterprise for the true ski mountaineer who does not wish to rely on a guide instead of exercising his own judgement. From this country guided HLR parties are arranged by the Ski Club of Great Britain (118 Eaton Square, London SW1 W9AF), by the Eagle Ski Club, and occasionally by the UK Section of the Austrian Alpine Club.

EQUIPMENT

Balancing overall weight against essential requirements calls for careful consideration beforehand and particularly affects the quantity of food carried (see hut notes).

1. CLOTHING

The harsher conditions of winter/spring stress the value of warm and windproof clothing. The extremities of the body require most attention: take strong mitts (also a reserve pair or at least gloves in addition), a balaclava, thick and thin pairs of knee-length woollen socks. A duvet jacket not only combats the cold outside but also has its use in unwardened huts and a windproof anorak or better a cagoule counteracts gales and snowfall. Long gaiters (the short variety are inadequate) keep the snow out of one's boots. Knee-length climbing breeches are far more practical than ski trousers. Woollen underwear is advisable. Do not forget (even with an overcast sky) to always use sunglasses or goggles, protective sun cream and lip salve: apply regularly because the sun's rays, reflected by the snow everywhere during the skiing season, burn one's face more quickly than is often appreciated. In this respect a peaked cap, preferably with let-down flaps to cover ears and the back of the neck, or a wide-brimmed hat acts as an extra shield.

2. MOUNTAINEERING

For ski touring purposes a 30 metre rope of 9mm. circumference generally suffices per party of two. Individuals should ideally take crampons, an ice axe, prussik loops or a seat harness or other more convenient gadgets (such as Jumar clamps) for crevasse rescue, and an avalanche cord. Make sure beforehand that crampons are adjusted to your ski boots. A few ice screws and karabiners can sometimes be useful and occasionally indispensable on the classic HLR.

3. SKIING

Metal, plastic or fibreglass SKIS (and combinations thereof) are preferable to plain wooden ones if financially possible. For touring, skis must be neither too rigid nor too heavy and neither too short nor too long. Lightweight skis such as the Kästle

CPM 70, the Rossignol Haute Route and the Blizzard Super Epoxi are ideal but expensive. Flexible skis can allow for uneven terrain and rigid models only realize their full potential in icy conditions or on hard pistes. Short skis, increasingly popular for teaching skiing to beginners, distribute one's weight over a smaller area and therefore increase the likelihood of breaking through surface crust or sinking into deep snow; however, in this range the Fischer Perfekt (1.70m.) has proved most reliable and is lighter than any full-length ski. In case of a breakage a party should equip itself with a spare ski tip. Langlauf skis are not to be considered.

Step-in BINDINGS with both toe and heel release offer the greatest security, but only a few types adapt satisfactorily to the needs of the tourer. The Vinersa Touromatic H model and the Marker M4 toe piece/Rotamat TR heel release are recommended. Bindings with a rigid heel release are useless for uphill movement because the boot sole cannot be raised. Many tourers still prefer a toe release combined with a safety cable unit (always carry a spare cable) and touring attachments. In this category the well designed Silvretta-Saas Fee-Alpin combination is the lightest model and cheaper than any other satisfactory binding. With either system bindings must be adjusted for ascent and descent. Retaining straps must be worn to prevent skis from soloing on downhill when a fall causes the bindings to open.

Long, light metal SKI STICKS with large baskets support one's weight best during an ascent, especially in deep snow. For the tourer, an ideal basket is not apparently marketed at present.

SKINS, nowadays made of synthetic fibres, are fixed on to the soles of one's skis for the ascent. The fibres are angled so that the ski slides forward comfortably, but not backwards. They must be fitted in advance. Modern skins are usually fastened at the tip of the ski. Always put them on tightly to stop snow getting between ski and skin. To avoid rapid abrasion both the tip fastener and side clips should be made of metal; the initial extra cost represents a long-term economy. Otherwise carry a repair kit. At present the reliable Vinersa patent tops the selling market, Vinersalpin being the most refined model. Trima skins can no longer be recommended; this once popular patent requires staples to be fitted to the groove of the ski sole, often a difficult task with slender modern skis. Although these skins are fastened most quickly, they defy proper repair if anything breaks and the staples can damage skis.

HARSCHEISEN, literally "crusted snow irons", are in fact ski crampons; these metal blades, attached to one's skis, facilitate the ascent of icy or steep slopes. They must be fitted very exactly in advance. They are useful, especially in late spring, but not essential.

Lace-up leather SKI BOOTS are undoubtedly far more practical than modern clip boots which are designed for the piste skier and are generally too rigid with a high shaft. In plastic boots one's feet cannot breathe properly and consequently they sweat. When ascending on foot the clips often come undone if crampons are not strapped on; they only have the advantage of being quickly adjustable. Several combined boots with a clip above the ankle are made by Swiss manufacturers. Only double boots give adequate protection against the cold.

The appropriate wax helps on a ski descent. Before setting off downhill check that lumps of ice have not formed on the running surface; this often explains why one's skis are not gliding smoothly.

For ski touring, a RUCKSACK should have detachable side pockets or side straps to simplify carrying skis (see note 4 on p. 28) and a waistband to prevent it swinging about during downhill runs.

4. GENERAL

Every individual or at the least every rational party should carry a map, compass, possibly an altimeter (an invaluable help in mist on vast glaciers), whistle (the international alpine distress signal is six blasts or other signals at ten-second intervals followed by a min. pause), torch, emergency rations and a full polythene bottle or thermos.

A bivouac sack and a first-aid kit should be carried. The weight and inconvenience involved obviously rule out full stretcher equipment. However, lightweight stretcher kits, utilizing the skis and sticks of the victim, are available. Repairs or adjustments to ski bindings can rarely be made without a screwdriver and possibly pliers. A lightweight snow shovel can be useful in an emergency for building a cave or an igloo and for avalanche rescue.

An insurance policy that covers helicopter rescue is a sound investment! The above notes indicate the main requirements but do not claim to be a complete kit list.

HUTS

Most huts are owned by the French, Swiss or Italian alpine clubs (CAF, SAC and CAI), a few privately. Relevant details concerning each establishment are given in Part II and not repeated in the HLR descriptions; they should be referred to as necessary, especially to pinpoint the position of a hut.

Huts are more primitive in winter and spring than in summer. Tourers accustomed to the comparative luxury of Austrian huts will be disappointed to find neither central heating nor washing facilities. Sleeping is entirely in dormitories with communal bunks. In SAC huts advance booking is officially required for large groups. Nearly all the huts on the HLR are wardened at least during a short part of the ski touring season and a very simple restaurant service is then provided. The timing of Easter affects the dates when the guardian is likely to be present and parties should therefore always carry adequate provisions or check the circumstances locally. Most huts now have a telephone; a surcharge above the normal tariff is levied on incoming and outgoing calls. The SAC and CAF huts listed here always remain at least partially and usually completely open. CAI huts generally leave a winter room, with only mattresses and blankets, open out of season; exceptions noted. Some huts become overcrowded around Easter and Whitsun, but in spring a full hut with a guardian can be preferable to an empty unwardened one where one must light the stove and melt snow at the end of a tiring day before preparing food or drink.

In winter/spring conditions straightforward access to huts should not be assumed. In certain cases approaches are threatened by avalanche danger. In addition, it should be

downhill parts: accidents can occur from individuals over-estimating their skiing ability and underestimating the steepness of a slope. The most convenient method of carrying skis requires a rucksack with detachable side pockets (or side straps): one ski is slotted upright between each side pocket and the main part of the rucksack, the bindings controlling the position of the skis, and the tips are bound together. Strapping skis across the top of a rucksack makes diagonal ascents and any descent most uncomfortable, apart from destroying one's sense of balance. The old-fashioned practice of dragging skis uphill, tied to a piece of rope, has long since been abandoned. Shouldering skis compromises one's balance by leaving only one hand free and is not recommended on steep ground. Irrespective of the method employed, rucksacks with skis on them do seem to have a will of their own!

5. Orientation. The directions "left" and "right" are used in the sense of direction of movement of the climber—ascent, descent, traverse of slope. Left and right banks of glaciers, rivers, gullies, etc., are identified in the direction of flow, i.e. downward. In ascent this means that the left bank of a glacier is on one's right hand. The direction is often confirmed by an abbreviated compass point.

APPROACHES AND TRANSPORT

N.B. Fares quoted apply in June 1973 and are subject to the regular fluctuations of the floating £ as well as inevitable international increases.

From Britain there are connecting train services by four channel routes across France via Paris and Le Fayet to Chamonix several times daily. The journey takes about 18 h. The best rail route to the Pennine Alps lies across France via Paris, Vallorbe to Lausanne, then along the Rhone valley to Brig. International express trains do not stop at Visp. Alight at Martigny for Verbier and Bourg St. Pierre, at Sion for Arolla, at Visp or Brig for Zermatt and Saas Fee. A Swiss Holiday Ticket, valid for one month, from London to Zermatt or Saas Fee, contains vouchers entitling the holder to make journeys during the course of the holiday at half price; these vouchers also procure smaller reductions on cableways. The journey takes about 19 h. From Basel or Zürich, travel by train to Chamonix via Bern and Geneva or via Lausanne, Martigny and the mtn. railway across the Col des Montets; for Brig the rail route goes via Bern and the Lötschberg tunnel.

Frequent flights from London Heathrow and Gatwick to Geneva take 1½ h. Geneva is the most conveniently situated international airport for onward travel to both Chamonix and the Pennine Alps.

Links with the Italian resorts on the S side of the Mont Blanc Range and Pennine Alps are provided by the Mont Blanc Road Tunnel (bus service from Chamonix to Courmayeur), the Great St. Bernard Road Tunnel (bus service from Martigny to Aosta) and the Simplon Rail Tunnel (train service from Brig to Domodossala, cars transported). From Turin a train service follows the Aosta valley to the railhead at Pré St. Didier, 5 km. S of Courmayeur; a more convenient direct coach service also operates. From Milan an international rail service connects with Brig via the Simplon tunnel.

A special daily connecting rail service operates between Zermatt and Chamonix, via Visp and Martigny; the journey takes about 5 h. Other resorts in the Pennine Alps are reached by regular bus services from the Rhone valley.

For motorists the quickest route also lies via Paris, reached by motorway either from Rouen (Newhaven-Dieppe cross channel service) or from Lille (Dover-Calais/Dunkerque). Continue by the Southern motorway to Beaune, then branch off through Poligny to Geneva or through Pontarlier to Lausanne. Toll on French motorways. On the whole ski tourers prefer public transport because thereby the commitment to return to a base is eliminated.

MAPS

The guidebook is designed for use with the official Swiss maps, the Landeskarte der Schweiz (LK)=Carte nationale de la Suisse (CN). French and less satisfactory Italian maps are available for some areas, but complicate the subject and no reference is made to them in the text. The Swiss maps, issued in three scales, cover both the Mont Blanc Range and the Pennine Alps.

For the conventional ski mountaineer the 1:50,000 scale series (LK 50) provides sufficient detail and forms the basis for all route descriptions here. The undermentioned maps are required to cover both ranges:

273	Montana	284	Mischabel (Zermatt-Saas Fee)
274	Visp	292	Courmayeur
282	Martigny	293	Valpelline
283	Arolla	294	Gressoney

Fortunately, only sheets 282, 283 and 284 are absolutely essential for the HLR; the version with ski routes, published on specially resistant syntosil paper and accompanied by brief descriptions on the reverse side, will be found invaluable. However, 293 should also be taken because the classic route overlaps slightly on to this sheet three times between Bourg St. Pierre and the Chanrion hut (line marked on 283). Similarly 294 covers important HLR alternatives on the Italian side of the Pennine Alps. 292 shows Mont Blanc and its immediate surroundings. No ski route versions have been issued for these last three sheets. 273 and 274 (ski route editions available) merely detail the N side approaches to the Pennine Alps and are not normally needed. Lastly, 2 special maps in 1:50,000 cover the ground of 282, 283, 284 plus the HLR excursions into 293. Sheets 5003, 5006, not available in ski route versions.

The newer 1:25,000 scale maps (LK 25) are useful for extra detail on complex terrain and meet the needs of the winter climber. Here they are only drawn upon for additional information. The appropriate sheets in connection with this guidebook are:

1326	Rosablanche	1345	Orsières
1328	Randa	1346	Chanrion
1329	Saas	1347	Matterhorn
1344	Col de Balme	1348	Zermatt

1349   Monte Moro   1365   Grand St. Bernard
                            1366   Mont Vélan

Two maps in the 1:100,000 series give a good overall impression of the HLR and its surroundings, including the Italian slopes:

46   Val de Bagnes   47   Monte Rosa

The new IGN 1:25,000 tourist map for the Mont Blanc Range, published in two sheets 231, 232 — and entitled Massif du Mont Blanc, supersedes all previous official French productions. Sheet 2 is required for the W limits of the range, summarized in Part V, which are also covered by a map in the IGN 1:50,000 grid series, St. Gervais-les-Bains XXXV-31. Another tourist map, similarly called Massif du Mont Blanc but on a 1:50,000 scale, is based on the IGN series and usefully indicates ski itineraries.

All these maps are sold in Britain by WEST COL PRODUCTIONS Goring Reading Berks England

ALTITUDES, NOMENCLATURE AND LANGUAGE

Altitudes are taken from the LK 50, referred to previously, unless otherwise indicated. Useful spot height references shown only on the newer LK 25 are quoted as well. Otherwise, where the map does not show an altitude it has usually been calculated from contour lines. It should be noted that heights of mtns., passes, huts, etc., are always in accordance with the LK 50 and not the LK 25 which has adjusted some altitudes, mainly downwards. The latest edition of the LK 50 occasionally indicates spot heights that do not appear on older editions or on the LK 50 ski map, and it has altered a few altitudes; moreover, a very small number of spot heights previously shown are inconveniently omitted. All altitudes and vertical intervals are expressed in metres.

Names are likewise taken primarily from the LK 50. Consequently French or German but not Italian names appear for frontier peaks and passes. Controversial and confusing revised spellings that appear on the newer LK 25 are ignored: often these merely represent local dialectal forms of terms. Where no name appears on the map it has been taken from a mountaineering publication, or in the case of "local" names acquired by personal knowledge.

A number of continental terms are used in the route descriptions. Most of those listed below have been incorporated into the English language (Oxford Dictionary) and are taken as understood: abseil, arête, bergschrund, col, couloir, crevasse, rognon, sérac, verglas.

The native language is German in the Saas and Zermatt valleys, but French in the Swiss valleys further W as well as in the Chamonix valley. English is widely spoken at all the major resorts on the N side of both the Mont Blanc Range and Pennine Alps. On the Italian side, however, surprisingly little English is spoken but French is generally understood.

LITERATURE

For further details about peaks merely summarized in Part V and for climbing as opposed to ski mountaineering consult the following Alpine Club guidebooks:

Selected Climbs in the *Mont Blanc Range* (2 Vols.) by R. G. Collomb and P. Crew, 1967.

Selected Climbs in the *Pennine Alps* (2 Vols.) by R. G. Collomb 1968.

Mont Blanc Range. Since 1976 this work has been published in 3 volumes. Mont Blanc itself is in Vol.I.

Pennine Alps. Since 1975 this work has been published in 3 volumes, viz. East, Central, West.

Also available in English language:
Chamonix-Mont Blanc. General visitors' guide.
Zermatt Area and Saas Fee. General visitors' guide.

Several continental publications on ski mountaineering relevant to the HLR are available. These include *Haute Route*, published in German, also *Mont Blanc-Gruppe*, and *Die Gipfelwelt der Haute*

Route (Roch), in French and German. In French, the SAC issues *Ski Alpin, Vol.3/Alpes Valaisannes*. These works treat the HLR in varying degrees, while the Roch book contains many photographs preceded by a substantial introduction.

The following books make interesting background or preparatory reading:
Alpine Ski Tour by R. Fedden
The Avalanche Enigma by C. Fraser
Mountaineering by A. Blackshaw
Ski by M. Heller
Handbook on Ski Touring and Glacier Skiing, Ski Club of Great Britain
Teach Yourself Skiing by M. Heller and M. Milne

CURRENCY

Wide exchange facilities exist at the major ski resorts only. Hoteliers will often oblige at a less favourable rate. The rate for presenting the wrong currency at huts is far worse. Present exchange rates are subject to the regular fluctuations of the market. The most convenient course of action is to carry adequate cash in French and Swiss Francs (and Italian Lire if required) with a reserve in travellers' cheques.

ACKNOWLEDGEMENTS

Donald Mill contributed very useful notes and also commented on the text. Robin Collomb checked the manuscript. Source reference material, including the loan of hundreds of magazines, documents and maps, was obtained from the West Col archives and Alpina Technica files at Goring on Thames. General information was supplied by Jules Carron, Henry Collomb, J. Hasler, Joan Pralong and several tourist offices. Plates A, C. F, J are reproduced by courtesy of the Swiss National Tourist Office. I thank the above-mentioned for their help.

(Ed. note. Since this was written Eric Roberts died on Annapurna I in 1979, and Donald Mill, his revision editor, was lost in an accident in Scotland a year later. The present revision has been done in-house at West Col Productions).

VALLEY BASES

These are treated from W to E and restricted to resorts relevant to route descriptions. Mechanized uphill transport that affects ski tours is noted here and detailed in the text.

1. VALLÉE DE CHAMONIX

The valley is served by railway and road from Geneva via Le Fayet to Chamonix (86 km.) and connects similarly with Martigny (38 km.) in Switzerland via Le Châtelard. The road across the Forclaz is now kept open in winter. An excellent bus service operates hourly at least within the confines of the valley and calls at all the mtn. cableway stations: Les Houches — Chamonix — Argentière — Le Tour. Both sides of the valley are served by an extensive network of cableways, chair lifts and ski tows. The main pistes offer superb runs for the competent skier, but are not suitable for beginners. Presentation of a CAF club card generally secures a ten per cent reduction on cableways, etc.

CHAMONIX-MONT BLANC (1041m.) (pop. 8500): The largest, busiest and most important mountaineering centre in the Alps. Road tunnel (toll, regular bus service) and unique cableway link with Courmayeur on the Italian side of the range. All classes of hotels, shops, guides' bureau, etc. Dormitory accommodation at the Refuge des Amis de la Montagne (room for self-cooking) behind the Montenvers station and at the Première de Cordée chalet near the Brévent lift terminus. Youth hostel at Les Pélerins 2½ km. from the town, near the tunnel fork road. The CAF office is situated near the main station. The Ecole Nationale de Ski et d'Alpinisme has its headquarters here. Snell Sports stock an outstanding selection of climbing and skiing equipment. The Aig. du Midi cableway starts from the Pélerins road on the SW outskirts; incidentally, contrary to French claims, the highest cableway in the world is not this one but another in the Venezuelan Andes.

ARGENTIÈRE (1257m.): This expanding village serves as the starting point for the classic HLR. Situated 8 km. NE of Chamonix. Hotels, shops, guides' bureau, etc. Dormitory and full board available at the Centre International d'Alpinisme (for over twenty-ones only), but often fully booked. Cableway in two stages to the Grands Montets.

LE TOUR (1453m.): A small village at the head of the 2 km. long slip road branching off R above Argentière. Railway station 1 km. below at Montroc (Mont Roch). Contractors' cableway towards the Albert Premier hut. Gondola lift to the Col de Balme.

2. SWISS VAL FERRET

From Orsières, connected by local railway with Martigny, the road up this valley breaks off S on the E side of the Mont Blanc Range to La Fouly (1593m.), the winter roadhead, infrequent bus service.

CHAMPEX (1466m.): A side road climbs in wide zigzags above Som la Proz on the W flank of the valley to this picturesque resort beside a lake, bus service (30 km. from Martigny). The road from Les Valettes is closed in winter. SAC restaurant. Reached upon completion of the first section of the classic HLR. Chair lift to La Breya.

3. VAL D'ENTREMONT

This valley leads from Martigny via Orsières up to the Great St. Bernard pass and flanks the W side of the Pennine Alps. The new road bypasses most settlements. Road tunnel (toll) under the pass to Italy (Aosta). A new skiing area has been developed above Bourg St. Bernard (1914m., not named on LK 50) near the tunnel entrance, known as Super St. Bernard.

BOURG ST. PIERRE (1632m.): An unfashionable village on the Great St. Bernard road 6 km. below the tunnel entrance, direct bus service from Martigny (32 km.). A few simple hotels and private accommodation. Many tourers patronize the Pension Au Beau Valais. The starting point for the Valsorey hut on the classic HLR.

4. VAL DE BAGNES

At Sembrancher (12 km. from Martigny) this valley branches E off the Great St. Bernard road. Access by local train from Martigny as far as Le Châble.

VERBIER (1490m.): A major ski resort with 30 different uphill transport systems, situated on a shelf above and N of the lower part of the valley. Much chalet accommodation. Connecting bus service from Le Châble. There is also a direct bus from Martigny (27 km.). A cableway now connects Le Châble to Verbier. The road zigzags steeply up to the village. Starting point for the Mont Fort hut and the most popular alternative to the classic HLR.

LOURTIER (1071m.): A small village with limited accommodation and shops. Starting point for the most reliable approach to the Panossière hut.

FIONNAY (1489m.): The village at the terminus of the winter/spring bus route from Le Châble (31 km. from Martigny). A few hotels and shops. Departure point for the Panossière and Chanrion huts (subject to suitable conditions). The road to Mauvoisin is closed until the snow melts and accommodation is not available there before June.

5. VAL D'HÉRENS

Breaks out of the Rhone valley at Sion.

AROLLA (1998m.): A new winter sports centre at the head of the upper W fork of the valley. The inevitable development of this superb skiing area commenced only recently; it has merely a few ski lifts at present. Hotels, shops, etc. Several establishments, incl. the Hotel du Pigne and the post office, provide dormitories with self-catering facilities. Access by bus, twice daily at least, from Sion (41 km.). The road is occasionally blocked by avalanches: in that case the bus service operates as far as Les Haudères. An excellent ski mountaineering base.

6. MATTERTAL

This is the W fork of the valley running S from Visp.

ZERMATT (1605m.): The most famous summer and winter resort in the Pennine Alps, at the foot of the Matterhorn. Access by mtn. railway from Visp or Brig, trains run about hourly. The new motor road has been completed to Täsch, the last train stop 6 km. before Zermatt (31 km. from Visp), huge car park. At present only local residents are permitted to drive up to Zermatt. All classes of hotels, shops, guides' bureau, etc. Provisions are most economically bought at the new Migros supermarket. The Hotel Bahnhof meets the requirements of the ski mountaineer with dormitories, a kitchen for self-catering guests, shower. Youth hostel above the R bank of the river near the Steinmatte-Winkelmatten path. A vast network of interconnecting mtn. transport is available to the skier with pistes to suit all standards. For the tourer the cableway system via Furi and Furgg to Trockener Steg, with a branch line to Schwarzsee, and the rack railway to Gornergrat, with a continuation cableway to the Stockhorn, greatly shorten approaches to huts and summits. Some parties terminate the HLR here. An ideal base for combining piste bashing with ski mountaineering and touring. Since 1981 the Trockener Steg-K1. Matterhorn lift has been open, also new lifts to the Furgggrat.

7. SAASTAL

The E branch of the valley S of Visp. Get off the train at

Stalden. In winter and spring the road in the valley floor is closed beyond Saas Almagell (1672m.).

SAAS FEE (1790m.): An important ski resort on a shelf above and W of the valley. Bus service from Stalden and directly from Visp (27 km.). Cars must be parked in the compound on the outskirts. All classes of hotels, shops, guides' bureau, etc. Reasonably priced rooms may be found on the Wildi road. Cableways to Felskinn and Längfluh virtually eliminate hut approaches. The end point of the HLR.

8. ITALIAN VALLEYS

They are rarely visited by British ski tourers, but were made more accessible in the 1960s by the opening of the Mont Blanc and Great St. Bernard road tunnels. Ski mountaineering possibilities are strictly limited in some valleys by unsuitable terrain.

Cervinia (Breuil) (2006m.) at the head of the Valtournanche connects with the Zermatt area by the Testa Grigia cableway, while Alagna (1190m.) in the Valsesia serves as the most convenient departure point for the Gnifetti hut and some of the Monte Rosa summits due to the Punta Indren cableway. Other resorts of possible interest are: Courmayeur and La Palud (departure point of cableway to the Pointe Helbronner and Chamonix) on the S side of the Mont Blanc Range, Gressoney-la Trinité (alternative approach to the Gnifetti hut) and Macugnaga at the S foot of the Monte Moro pass.

Accommodation is found in all the villages mentioned. Camping is not practical in spring, and in any case the ski tourer is seldom committed to a specific base.

Summer (piste) skiing facilities are located at the top of cableway systems on the Géant, Grands Montets, Theodul, Fee and Indren glaciers. Many others are being developed.

Further general information, including brochures that list all uphill transport systems and official ski runs, is available from local tourist offices on the spot or from national tourist offices:

French Government Tourist Office, 178 Piccadilly, London W1V 0AL.

Italian State Tourist Dept., 201 Regent Street, London W1.

Swiss National Tourist Office, Swiss Centre, 1 New Coventry Street, London W1V 3HG.

PART II

HUTS

Described from W to E. Notes are given for each hut on the situation, number of places, and facilities. Opening details do not apply to the summer season when almost all the huts have a resident warden. Approaches to huts on the HLR are described for those who wish to join the tour at any stage or are forced to break off due to bad weather, etc. Huts in areas or on mtn. routes merely summarized in Part V are excluded here but are detailed in the last part of the guide.

Vallot Hut   4362m.
Refuge Vallot—Mont Blanc.   Property of the CAF Paris-Chamonix Section. This duralumin shelter with 24 places is situated on the Foudroyés rocks near the foot of the Bosses ridge. It is principally intended for emergency use and has saved many parties; conversely, beware of getting trapped here during prolonged bad weather. Despite the repeated renewal of equipment do not rely on finding usable blankets and mattresses. The nearby Vallot observatory is locked and closed to the public.

For access see Route 39.

Grands Mulets Hut   3051m.
Refuge des Grands Mulets.   Property of the CAF Paris-Chamonix Section. Tel. (50) 53 16 98.   Built as a replacement in 1960 on the lowest of the three rock islands above the junction of the Taconna(z) and Bossons glaciers.   70 places, resident warden from Easter onwards according to the snow conditions, check up at the guides' bureau in Chamonix. Sometimes overcrowded at weekends in late spring, especially Whitsun.

The first part of the approach from the Plan de l'Aiguille is exposed to avalanche danger after snowfall and the ascent to the hut should only be undertaken after such snow has stabilized. The state of the route around la Jonction varies considerably and skis may have to be carried in places. Ladders are normally positioned across the largest crevasses. The modern approach from the Plan de l'Aiguille cableway station is described below. The traditional routes from the valley are no longer used due to the availability of the cableway, but if sufficient snow remains, it is possible in descent to ski directly and very steeply down to the Mont Blanc tunnel entrance from the Gare des Glaciers or to Chamonix on the piste from the Plan de l'Aiguille. However suitable conditions for an ascent of Mont Blanc rarely coincide with snow down to the valley; consequently most parties also go down by the cableway.

It is possible to take the cableway from the Plan de l'Aiguille up to the Aig. du Midi, then ski down the Vallée Blanche (see p. 108), a splendid finale after an ascent of Mont Blanc.

1 From Chamonix take the Aig. du Midi cableway to the intermediate station at the Plan de l'Aiguille (2310m.) (small reduction upon presentation of any alpine club card).

Start SE but soon head S on to the Pélerins glacier which is crossed almost horizontally to the SW at c.2370m. Continue in the same direction below the NW face of the Aig. du Midi to the derelict cableway station of the Gare des Glaciers (2414m.).

The next section to the Bossons glacier crosses several gullies and short steep slopes which in unfavourable conditions are subject to avalanches and stonefall. At first head up the moraine towards the Aig. du Midi, then traverse SW to gain the R bank of the Bossons glacier at c.2500m. Cross the glacier by a prominent terrace SW to la Jonction, above the last islands of the Montagne de la Côte. Here the route is complicated by innumerable crevasses and séracs. Head up steep slopes towards the Grands Mulets rocks, turning difficulties R. The slope eases and broadens by (W of) the rock island. Skis can be left at the foot of the rocks. Go up a path with an iron handrail from R to L to the hut (4-4½ h. from the Plan de l'Aiguille).

Albert Premier Hut   2702m.
Refuge Albert Premier. Property of the CAF Paris-Chamonix

Section. A modern hut situated on the R bank of the Tour glacier. 128 places. From Easter onwards the guardian is usually present at least at weekends and provides a restaurant service. Radio telephone. The old hut immediately below otherwise remains open.

The shortest summer approach from the top station of the Col de Balme lift, contouring below the Charamillon lake to a shoulder on the W ridge of the Pointe des Berons (de Bron), is very exposed to avalanches in winter/spring and rarely practical before late May. Even the summer route from Le Tour is often doubtful from 1600m. to 2200m. and here a safer line is taken a little to the S nearer the Pissoir (P(i)cheu) stream according to the conditions.

From Le Tour a contractors' cableway rises to c.2050m. on the R lateral moraine of the Tour glacier and this will eventually be made available to the public. Its opening will greatly simplify access to the hut for ski tourers and is bound to increase the popularity of this approach to the Trient plateau, both for the HLR and the Three Cols Traverse. Still not open in 1984.

2   From Le Tour (1453m.) ascend gentle open slopes E. These soon steepen appreciably. At first keep near the Pissoir stream (named thus on LK 25), but by c.1700m. at the latest cross an old moraine R and head towards the inaccessible tongue of the Tour glacier, more like an icefall, until a steep cwm opens on the L and leads ENE up to the R lateral moraine of the Tour glacier at c.2200m. In places skis are best carried. Now continue up or near the moraine ridge to the hut (4 h.).

N.B. In descent this route does not normally give a pleasant ski run.

For the Trient hut see routes 27 and 14 ($2\frac{1}{2}$h.).

Argentière Hut   2771m.
Refuge d'Argentière. Situated on the R bank of the Argentière glacier at the SW foot of the Aig. d'Argentière below the ridge that separates the Milieu and Améthystes glaciers. Property of the CAF Paris-Chamonix Section. 140 places. Tel.(50)53-16-92. Guardian present at Easter, Whitsun and weekends in spring. Otherwise the hut remains partially open with 50 places

available. N.B. The reconstruction and substantial enlargement of this hut in 1974 was assisted by the Alpine Club in return for which its members received reciprocal rights in all CAF huts.

For the approach from the Grands Montets cableway terminus or Argentière see Route 11. Connections to other huts are as follows: Albert Premier by the Three Cols Traverse, page 84. Trient, Route 14. A Neuve, Route 28(a). Orny, Route 13.

Trient Hut   3170m.

Cabane du Trient. Situated on the R bank of the Plateau du Trient below and S of the Pointe d'Orny. Property of the SAC Diablerets Section. Recently enlarged, 155 places. Tel. (026) 41438. No warden in winter/spring as most parties bypass the hut. All approaches are long and require reasonable snow conditions. Diagram on p. 60.

Both routes from Champex are described in descent: see Routes 15, 12 and 13 as well as the Stage 8 note to the HLR East to West on p. 81. Surprisingly, the quickest way to the hut from Le Tour by the Grands glacier to the Plateau du Trient, as described briefly on p. 83, is hardly used (4 h.). For the strenuous approach from Trient and La Forclaz either by the R bank of the Trient glacier or, more roundabout, by the Grands glacier allow 6-8 h. In descent the latter route can give a superb ski run. For the traverse from the Argentière hut see Route 14. From the Albert Premier hut see Route 27.

A Neuve Hut   2735m.

Cabane de l'A Neuve. Situated on the L bank of the Neuve glacier below the Pointes des Essettes. Unwardened in winter/spring. Property of the SAC Diablerets Section. 26 places.

According to the snow conditions avalanche danger is sometimes considerable on the ski approach from La Fouly, described in descent under Route 28(b) (3½-4 h. in ascent), and the hut is seldom visited before late spring. For the traverse from the Argentière hut see Route 28(a). Tel.(026) 42424.

Orny Hut   2826m.

Cabane d'Orny. Situated on the L bank of the Orny glacier

above its tongue. Property of the SAC Diablerets Section. Tel. (026) 41887. No warden in winter/spring. 75 places.

This new hut is passed by parties following the descent variant to Orsières on Stage 2 of the HLR: see Route 13 and the Stage 8 note to the HLR East to West on p. 81. For the traverse from the Albert Premier hut combine Routes 27 and 13.

Valsorey Hut   3030m.

Cabane de Valsorey. Property of the SAC La Chaux-de-Fonds Section. Situated on a small promontory at the top of a long rock spur on the SW side of the Grand Combin massif. Fine view of Mont Vélan to the S. 36 places. Warden sometimes present from late March onwards. Tel. (026) 49122.

For the approach from Bourg St. Pierre see Route 16. The hut can be reached from the Panossière hut by crossing the Col du Meitin: see Routes 30 and 40 N.B.1 (5-5½ h.), serious.

Mont Fort Hut   2457m.

Cabane du Mont Fort. Situated in a prominent position on a knoll above the Chaux pastures and S of the Col du Mont Gelé. Property of the SAC Jaman Section. Warden usually present in spring, simple restaurant service. 100 places. Tel. (026) 79384.

The cableways and ski lifts above Verbier have greatly simplified access to this hut without seriously reducing the choice of ski tours up to now. In fact the cableway from Tortin to the Col de Chassoure has opened up the N side ski runs in the Mont Fort-Rosablanche group and made day round trips practical. However, the projected cableway systems to the Mont Fort would alter this situation, but construction is not anticipated for some years yet. The first of the approaches described below in order of convenience and reliability is best when laden with a heavy rucksack. Times quoted exclude the lift journeys.

3 (a) From the upper (E) end of Verbier (1529m.) take the lift up to Les Ruinettes (2194m.), then the Tête des Ruinettes ski tow from 2200m. to 2258m. and, after a very brief run NE, the Combe ski tow from 2200m. to 2460m. Head NE along the broad crest to pt.2466m., known as the Col de Médran, in a few

min. and traverse almost horizontally E, later SE to the hut
(¾ h.). Red poles with arrows mark the route.

(b) Take the cableway via Les Ruinettes and Les Attelas to
Mont Gelé (3023m.). Ski steeply down the SE ridge on a piste,
only open in safe conditions (check beforehand), to the Col du
Mont Gelé (2804m.) and S over broader slopes to the hut (½ h.).
This run should be undertaken by proficient skiers exclusively.

(c) Take the cableway via Les Ruinettes to Les Attelas
(2727m.), using the R-hand lift on the second section to arrive
nearer the Col des Vaux (2708m.). Traverse the lower slopes
of the W flank of Mont Gelé (avalanche danger at times) downwards to cross its SW ridge at c.2580m. and ski SE to the hut
(¾-1 h.).

(d) Few if any parties ascend the piste from Verbier via Le
Mayentset, the Vacheret slopes and the Médran basin to join
(a) at the top of the Combe ski tow (3½ h. to the hut). This is the
descent route.

(e) The approach by the steep SW slopes, first passing
through various small hamlets, from Sarreyer (1239m.), situated
at the end of a side road NW above Lourtier, might occasionally
interest parties who have returned to the Val de Bagnes from
the Panossière hut (4-4½ h.).

Brunet Hut   2103m.
Cabane Marcel Brunet. Now indicated and named on LK 50.
Property of the Fédération Montagnarde Genevoise. Situated
N of the Petit Combin and NNE of the nearby Sery chalet
(2233m.) on a terrace due W of Fionnay in the Val de Bagnes.
The hut is passed on the way from Lourtier to the Panossière
hut. 32 places. Guardian rarely present except at weekends,
door otherwise locked, collect the keys at Champsec from the
guardian. To the SW of the hut Mont Rogneux, the Grand
Laget and the Pointe de Boveyre provide fairly short ski tours
(about 3 h. each), suitable outings when the higher peaks around
the Panossière hut are not in condition.

For the approach see Route 4.

Panossière Hut   2671m.
Cabane de Panossière. Situated on the R lateral moraines of the

Corbassière glacier at the W foot of the Grand Tavé. A new hut built by the SAC Geneva Section in 1969 about 100m. NW of the old hut which remains locked. Warden usually present during the ski touring season from Easter onwards, simple restaurant service. 100 places. In the Western Pennines this hut is nowhere surpassed for ski mountaineering possibilities, serving as the starting point for the Grand Combin and a varied selection of fine ski peaks. Very few parties undertake the long traverse to the Chanrion hut. Tel. (026) 75464.

In early spring by far the safest way to the hut leads from Lourtier via the Brunet hut and the Col des Avouillons. The shorter approach from Fionnay (Plan Pro) requires good snow conditions or little snow, especially below Plan Goli, and is otherwise subject to avalanche danger.

4   From Lourtier (1071m.) cross the River Drance de Bagnes and ascend the summer track first SW, later SE (zigzag movements) past Le Rosay to the Tougne (mis-spelt on map) chalets (1630m.). N.B. Alternatively come up to this point by a longer roundabout route from Champsec or, better, leave the road half-way between Lourtier and Fionnay by pt.1333m. (parking space) to take a path that traverses W to join the above approach near Pléna Dzeu (shorter). From here a jeep track leads to hut.

Now continue SE up the wooded slopes to pt.1844m., a forest clearing with one chalet, and zigzag up steeper open slopes in the same direction to the Brunet hut (2103m.). This hut remains invisible from below, but a pole indicates its location (3-3½ h.).

Head SSW to the Sery chalet (2233m.) and somewhat illogically go SW up to La Chaux and S to the Pindin chalet before descending ESE to pt.2232m. in the narrow Diure de Sery valley basin. A direct horizontal traverse S from the Sery chalet between small rock outcrops to this point can be unpleasant. Ascent SE to pt.2336m. and then keep initially to the gentler slopes below the N foot of the Avouillons ridge on the R-hand side of the basin leading up to the Col des Avouillons (2649m.). Curve slightly L and finally climb directly to the col (2½ h.).

On the other side descend steeply ESE, normally on foot at first in the broad couloir, to the Corbassière glacier. Occasional avalanche danger here. Follow its L(W) bank to c.2640m. and cross the glacier L(E) above a crevasse zone to the hut on the R bank moraines. It is equally possible to cross to the R bank moraines well below the crevasse zone (1½ h., 4 h. from the Brunet hut, 7-7½ h. from Lourtier).

5　Leave the Fionnay road after the second bend beyond Plan Pro at the Mayen du Revers (bus stop, named on LK 25 only, just below road spot height pt.1433m. on LK 50) and zigzag SW up sparsely wooded slopes. Soon head SE up to the Marduet clearing. N.B. Once the slopes are clear of snow reach this point from Fionnay (1489m.) on the signposted summer path. Now traverse W to the Corbassière chalets at pt.1959m. Go SE on the Corbassière crest or its W side to pt.2108m. and make a downward traverse S below rocks to pt.2004m. in the valley basin below the snout of the Corbassière glacier (pole markers). Ascend SE to the R bank moraine of the glacier (the LK 50 ski map does not show post-war recession) at the N edge of Plan Goli near pt.2232m. N.B. The traverse across steep slopes to Plan Goli, taking the same line as the summer path and marked as the ski route on the LK 50 ski map, should only be attempted in safe snow conditions. From Plan Goli follow the R lateral moraine of the Corbassière glacier in a R-hand curve past pt.2524.4m. to the hut (4½-5½ h.).

Few parties return to the valley by crossing the Col de Panossière to the Great St. Bernard road between Liddes and Bourg St. Pierre: see Stage 7 note to the HLR East to West on p. 81. As an approach particularly strenuous (8½-10 h.).
For the connection from the Valsorey hut by the Col du Meitin see Routes 30 and 40 (about 3½ h.); pointless unless abandoning the classic HLR for the sake of the Grand Combin. To the Valsorey hut allow 5-5½ h. For the serious traverse to the Chanrion hut see Route 30.

Prafleuri Hut　2662m.
Cabane de Prafleuri. Privately owned, this renovated hut was originally built as a barrack by the contractors for the Grande Dixence hydro-electric scheme. Situated on a terrace at the

head of the Prafleuri cwm near pt.2662m. E of the tongue of the Prafleuri glacier and due W of Mont Blava. 40 places but only a room with 18 places remains permanently open, no guardian.

Direct access from the Hérémence (Dix) valley in winter/spring is difficult and dangerous (avalanches). An approach from or bad weather exit to the Nendaz (Cleuson) valley via the Col de Prafleuri always remains possible and has become far more practical due to the cableway link between Tortin and Verbier. However, this hut serves its principal purpose as an optional intermediate stopping point on the long traverse from the Mont Fort hut to the Dix hut: see Route 31(ii). Popular with guided parties.

Chanrion Hut   2460m.
Cabane de Chanrion. Property of the SAC Geneva Section. Situated in the heart of the Western Pennines above the head of the Val de Bagnes on a small plateau at the SW foot of the Pointe d'Otemma. Tel. (026) 79209.   Warden, 100 places.

In winter/spring the hut serves almost exclusively as a stopping point on the HLR between the Valsorey and Vignettes huts. Direct access from the Val de Bagnes by the W bank of the Mauvoisin lake poses a serious problem and remains impractical or at least very dangerous until late spring in a normal season. Information about the prevailing conditions should be obtained from the attendant at the barrage by telephone: (026) 72203.

This is the worst place to be caught in prolonged bad weather and in such circumstances parties must on no account attempt to force a direct descent to the valley. Instead, either traverse to Arolla via the Vignettes hut (Routes 18 and 8) or the Dix hut (Routes 33 and 7), or cross the Fenêtre de Durand to Ollomont in Italy (Stage 7 note to the HLR East to West on p. 81).

6   The road between Fionnay (1489m.) and Mauvoisin (1840m.) is officially closed in winter/spring and impassable other than on foot/ski (1½-2 h.). Above Mauvoisin the road continues to the W side of the barrage. Then walk through a tunnel for nearly 1 km. (If this is blocked by snow, then a traverse to the S of the steep Pierre à Vire rocks immediately above the dam wall is not to be contemplated.) Follow the W bank of the lake (jeep track, two short tunnels) which is seriously exposed to avalanches as long as much snow remains on the slopes above. Beyond the lake go along the W bank of the stream, cross the Lancet bridge (2041m.) L, then keep to the E bank or valley bed to reach the head of the Chermotane basin near pt.2206m. and ascend gentle slopes N to the hut. Or, when the direct track from the Lancet bridge begins to clear of snow, climb it by numerous zigzags between minor rock barriers to the hut ($3\frac{1}{2}$-5 h. from Mauvoisin, 5-7 h. from Fionnay).

For the connection with the Valsorey hut see Route 17. For the Vignettes hut see Route 18 or 19. For the Dix hut see Route 33. For the Panossière hut see Route 30.

Dix Hut   2928m.
Cabane des Dix. Situated above the L bank of the Cheilon glacier on a detached hump immediately below and S of the rock knoll of the Tête Noire. Property of the SAC Monte Rosa Section. Warden normally resident in spring from late March onwards, simple restaurant service,145 places. Tel. (027)811523.

The alternative summer approach from Le Chargeur (the Hérémence/Dix valley road remains closed beyond Mâche) below the Dix dam wall is dangerous in winter/spring conditions and the tunnels on the W bank of the lake are normally blocked by snow. The safest route crosses the Pas de Chèvres from Arolla and is shortened by a ski lift.

7   From the post office at Arolla (1998m.) start WSW through the forest past the Hotel Kurhaus (2067m.) (building developments and access road) and the Tsidjiore Nouve huts to the open slopes by the L bank moraine of the Tsidjiore Nouve glacier. Continue up the wide valley in the same direction and beyond the small plateau at pt.2516m. head W over steeper slopes to the Pas de Chèvres (2855m.) ($2\frac{1}{2}$-3 h.).

It is in fact now customary practice to use the new Fontanesses ski lift and thereby save $1\frac{1}{2}$ h. This tow is now marked on the map and its valley station lies at c.1980m. just S of Arolla and immediately above the road. The upper terminus at c.2510m. is situated approx. 250m. SE of pt.2516m. Reach the Pas de Chèvres as above in 1-1½ h.

On the other side climb down a 15m. rock face by means of two iron ladders. Slant briefly L down to the E bank of the Cheilon glacier and make a gently rising traverse SW to the opposite bank, finally reaching the hut from the S by a L-hand curve (1 h., 2-2½ h. from the Fontanesses ski lift, 3½-4 h. from Arolla).

Fine ski traverses connect with the Mont Fort hut (Route 31), the Prafleuri hut (Route 31(ii)), the Vignettes hut (Route 32) and the Chanrion hut (Route 33).

Singla Bivouac Hut   3180m.
Bivouac de l'Aiguillette à la Singla. M████d Biv. on the map. Built in 1969 by the SAC Chasseron Section, more like a small hut with 12 places and 30 blankets. Situated half-way between the Chanrion and Vignettes huts well above the L bank of the Otemma glacier on the S ridge of the Aiguillette rock island (3198.7m.) which rises NNW of the Bec de la Sasse between the Aiguillette glacier to the W and the Blanchen glacier to the E.

No warden, door unlocked, a comfortable shelter insulated inside with cork, fully equipped, primus stove (fuel in reserve) and gas stove (possible no spare cartridges).

For access from the Otemma glacier see the introduction to Route 18.

Vignettes Hut   3157m.
Cabane des Vignettes. Situated at the E foot of the Pigne d'Arolla about 200m. E of the Col des Vignettes just on the S side of the rock ridge and above an impressive drop to the glacier below. Property of the SAC Monte Rosa Section. Enlarged 1972/73. Warden throughout spring, simple restaurant service, 128 places. Tel. (027)831322. The convergence here of the HLRs from Bourg St. Pierre and Verbier to Zermatt, added

to the popularity of the Pigne d'Arolla, make this hut the most frequented in the Pennine Alps W of Zermatt.

Using the Fontanesses ski lift involves taking a roundabout route that nevertheless reduces the time required to reach the hut. In conjunction with the development of Arolla as a winter sports centre the likely construction of further lifts in the vicinity may soon create softer options for approaching this hut. Three alternative starts are described below.

8 (a) From just S of Arolla take the Fontanesses ski lift to the top station at c.2510m., situated approx. 250m. SE of pt. 2516m. Ski SE across the Tsidjiore Nouve glacier moraines, losing about 50m. Then slant ESE up to the L bank moraine crest of the Pièce glacier near pt.2563m. below the Lettès Econdoi rock ridge.

(b) From the post office at Arolla (1998m.) start WSW through the forest past the Hotel Kurhaus (2067m.) (building developments and access road) to the Tsidjiore Nouve huts (piste) before crossing the line of the Fontanesses ski lift L(S) to the former L bank moraine of the Tsidjiore Nouve glacier. Continue S across this to the L bank moraine of the Pièce glacier which is followed SSW up to pt.2563m. to join (a).

(c) From the Mont Collon hotel at Arolla go S along the road for c.250m. to the bottom station of the Fontanesses ski lift (see (a) above) before breaking off SW up sparsely wooded slopes (piste) to join approach (b) at c.2200m. New skitow.

Now slant L(S) on to the Pièce glacier. Go up its L(W) bank, trending towards the centre at c.2800m. or over to the opposite bank according to the state of the crevasses (normally concealed). Reach the Col des Vignettes by a steeper slope and bear L(E) along the short ridge to the hut (3-3½ h. from the Fontanesses lift, 4-4½ h. from Arolla).

N.B. The descent to Arolla gives a splendid ski run.

Connections with other huts are as follows: Chanrion, Route 18 or 19. Dix, Route 32. Bertol, note on p. 94. Schönbiel, Route 20.

Bertol Hut 3311m.
Cabane de Bertol. New hut built 1976, situated on a shoulder

of the Clocher de Bertol buttress immediately N of the Col de Bertol. Superb view of the Dent Blanche. The stopping point on the Arolla-Zermatt HLR. Warden, meals, 80 places. Property of the SAC Neuchâtel Section. Tel. (027)831929.

On no account attempt to follow the line of the summer track up to the Plans de Bertol. Immediately below Mont Collon the route is exposed to avalanches from the N face above, and in poor snow conditions the upper part of the Bertol glacier becomes avalanche prone.

Motorists should not park their cars near the helicopter landing pad by the Grande Dixence pumping station (2008m.), situated half-way between Arolla and the summer roadhead near foot of the glacier.

9 From the Mont Collon hotel at Arolla follow the road, which is kept open to the Grande Dixence pumping station even in winter, on the L bank of the Borgne stream towards the Lower Arolla glacier snout and head SSE up the glacier to the N foot of Mont Collon. Bear L(E) and climb more steeply by a narrower slope to the Upper Arolla glacier, keeping away from the N face of Mont Collon on the R. Continue the L-hand arc immediately below pt.2521m. (omitted on new LK 50, c.400m. SE of pt.2615.6m.) so as to head N across a terrace off the glacier and up to the Plans de Bertol bivouac hut (2665m.), a primitive SAC shelter (2½-3 h.).

Now ascend NE, taking the same line as the summer path, to the Bertol glacier and make for the rognon in the centre of the glacier at c.3000m. (The most obvious opening ahead on its L is the Col de la Tsa.) Climb the cwm on the R and the steep slopes above E to the Col de Bertol (3269m.). Go briefly L to the foot of the Clocher de Bertol buttress where skis can be left. Climb the steep rocks, using fixed chains which may be iced up, to the hut (2½-3 h., 5-6 h. from Arolla, ½ h. less from the Grande Dixence pumping station).

For the traverse to the Schönbiel hut and Zermatt see Routes 34 and 20. For the connection with the Vignettes hut see note on p. 94.

Schönbiel Hut   2694m.

Schönbielhütte. Situated on a terrace above the L bank moraine and the confluence of the Schönbiel and Zmutt glaciers, opposite the N face of the Dent d'Hérens. Property of the SAC Monte Rosa Section. Tel. (028)671354. Warden occasionally present in late spring. 85 places.

Reached from Zermatt in 4½ h. by reversing the last part of Route 20. To shorten access appreciably, take the cableway to Schwarzsee (2582m.) and start down the Weisse Perle ski run before breaking off WNW at c.2450m. to cross the Hörnli ski lift and the Obere Stafelalp slopes downwards to the Zmutt glacier moraines (2½ h. from Schwarzsee to the hut); see Route 22 also. The traverse to the Vignettes hut is described in reverse under Route 20. For the Bertol hut combine Routes 20 and 34.

Theodul Hut   3317m.

Rifugio Teodulo. Situated on the rock shoulder immediately N of the Theodulpass (3290m.) on the frontier ridge. Property of the CAI Torino Section. 65 places. Officially open throughout spring with a full restaurant service, but the presence of the guardian cannot be guaranteed and in his absence the hut remains locked; inquire locally. Alternative accommodation may be available at the Testa Grigia cableway terminus. The importance and use of this hut has greatly declined due to the network of cableways and ski lifts that now cover both the Swiss and Italian approaches.

From the S end of Zermatt (near Winkelmatten) take the cableway via Furi and Furgg to Trockener Steg (2939m.), then the Gandegg and Theodulpass ski tows. From Cervinia (Breuil, 2006m.) the hut is reached by taking the cableway via Plan Maison to the Testa Grigia (3479m.) and skiing N down the piste to the Theodulpass. A ski tow operates between the Theodulpass and the Testa Grigia. Ski runs down to Zermatt are detailed under Route 43. Kl. Matterhorn lift alternatives.

For the connection from the Schönbiel hut and to the Monte Rosa hut see Route 22. For traverses to the Monte Rosa hut, incl. ways off to the Quintino Sella and Gnifetti huts, by the Italian HLR see Routes 35 and 36.

Monte Rosa Hut   2795m.
Monte Rosahütte or Bétempshütte. Situated on the Lower
Plattje rocks immediately above the R bank moraine of the
Grenz glacier and at the NW foot of the Monte Rosa group.
This important hut serves as the base for the largest selection
of long high altitude ski tours in the Alps. Property of the
SAC Monte Rosa Section. Tel. (028)672115. Resident warden
and staff with full restaurant service from mid-March onwards.
100 places. By installing two-tier bunks in some dormitories 35
extra places are to be created.

The traditional approach and alternative ways to the hut are
described under Route 21 and the preamble to Stage 7 of the
HLR respectively. For the traverse to the Britannia hut see
Route 23. From the Theodul hut see Routes 22, 35 and 36.

Gnifetti Hut   3611m.
Capanna Gnifetti. Situated on the upper rocks of the long rib
between the Lis and Garstelet glaciers. Property of the CAI
Varallo Section. This enlarged modern hut has been wardened
in spring since the construction of the cableway from Alagna to
the Punta Indren upper terminus at 3260m. on the ridge dividing
the Indren and Bors glaciers. 200 places, hotel service.

Reach the hut in 1½-2 h. from the lift terminus by crossing the
Indren glacier NW before ascending a rock barrier by a L-hand
curve to the small Garstelet glacier (unnamed on LK 50). The
longer approach from Gressoney-la Trinité has been shortened
recently by lifts to the Colle d'Olen which provide the link with
the Alagna skiing area (further projects towards the Gnifetti
hut under consideration).

This hut is the only popular ski mountaineering base on the
Italian side of the Pennine Alps and forms the ideal starting-
point for all the minor Monte Rosa summits, of which the
Piramide Vincent (4215m.) is the easiest.

Margherita Hut   4556m.
Capanna Regina Margherita. This hut on the summit of the
Signalkuppe at the head of the Grenz glacier is the highest in
the Alps. New monstrous building in 1980, three storeys high,
warden and meals, very expensive, 70 places. Property of the CAI

Central Committee. Radio telephone. For skiers, a trap in prolonged bad weather. Adequate clothing should be taken to combat the cold.

See Route 45 to the Signalkuppe for the approach from the Monte Rosa hut; this includes a note on access from the Gnifetti hut.

Längfluh Inn   2870m.
Hotel Längfluh. Situated a few min. above the upper terminus of the Saas Fee-Spielboden-Längfluh cableway. Owned by the Saas Fee Commune. Tel. (028) 48132. Open from December throughout the skiing season with full restaurant service. Dormitory, 100 places. The best starting-point for the Alphubel and Allalinhorn, but these ascents are often made directly from the valley by travelling up on the first cableway of the day or by parties based on the Britannia hut.

The direct piste descent to Saas Fee gives a steep ski run. Alternatively first ascend S and cross the Fee glacier E above its icefall before skiing down below pt.3081m. to join the easier Felskinn piste (Route 26). For the connection with the Britannia hut reverse Route 38.

Britannia Hut   3029m.
Britanniahütte. This modernized and enlarged hut is situated in the gap at the E end of the Hinter Allalin ridge between the Kessjen and Hohlaub glaciers. 113 places. Property of the SAC Geneva Section. Originally built with a subscription from the Association of British Members of the SAC in 1912. Tel. (028)572288. Warden with restaurant service from early March onwards.

Access has been simplified by the Felskinn cableway which is nowshown on the LK 50 ski map; further ski lifts are planned in the vicinity of the upper terminus. See Route 26 for the descent to Saas Fee.

10   The valley station of the Felskinn cableway (1840m.) at Bifig lies SSW of Saas Fee (1790m.) and is reached by a 15 min. walk along an asphalt road through Kalbermatten. As long as the ground remains snow-covered, a convenient ski tow provides uphill transport here. Travel by the cableway to the Felskinn terminus (2990m.) on a rock island W of the Egginerjoch.

Ascend briefly S and traverse the slope almost horizontally E, above a crevassed zone that is marked off by flags and ropes, to the Egginerjoch (2991m.). Then cross the upper slopes of the small Kessjen glacier SE to the hut. In poor visibility by keeping near the foot of the Hinter Allalin rocks on the R one can virtually eliminate all risk of missing the hut (¾-1 h.).

For the traverse to the Monte Rosa hut follow Route 48 to the Adlerpass and then reverse Route 23. For the connection with the Längfluh inn see Route 38.

Bouquetins Bivouac Hut   2980m.
New in 1975, situated on moraine forming a broad hump and prominent corner where the Haut Arolla gl. bends in descent from NW to N, on its true R bank. Door open, no warden, utensils, etc., stove for cooking but simpler to use your own, places for 15. Easily the most important recent amenity to the classic HLR. It breaks the long Stage 6, Route 20, into two more endurable parts. Coming from Arolla, approach as for Route 9 and continue S with a few crevasse obstacles up the main gl. to hut (3½ h.).

Pantalons Blancs Bivouac Hut   3280m.
New in 1975, situated on a small rock island halfway up a gl. spur dividing the Ecoulais and Pantalons Blancs gls, almost due W of and above S end of Dix lake. Door open, no warden, stove, etc., places for 15. Serves secondary ascents and crossings in the Rosablanche group. Route 31 (iii) comes nearest to the hut.

PART III

CLASSIC HIGH LEVEL ROUTE

In this section the classic HLR is described as a continuous traverse from Chamonix (Argentière) via Champex, Bourg St. Pierre and Zermatt to Saas Fee. Variants are detailed as appropriate after each stage, while alternative high level routes (that link up with the classic HLR) are dealt with comprehensively in Part IV.

Most circumstances favour a traverse of the HLR from W to E, the line adopted in this guidebook, and the pioneers took this direction. In either direction modern cableways now shorten the first stage considerably. Going from W to E undoubtedly gives better downhill skiing and enables most of the short steep sections normally done on foot to be taken in ascent. The Fenêtre du Chamois (Stage 2) forms an exception to this, but it can be avoided and in any case is offset by the subsequent fine ski run down the Arpette valley.

The chief disadvantage from E to W lies in having to descend parts on foot with a consequent loss of downhill skiing: namely the W slope of the Adlerpass, the W slope of the Col du Mont Brulé, and above all the problem of getting down to the Valsorey hut from the Plateau du Couloir which is much more serious in descent and more dangerous late in the day. In addition the ski runs down to the valley from the Monte Rosa and Valsorey huts are rarely enjoyable. The stage from the Schönbiel hut to the Vignettes hut is strenuous and longer than any stage on the W to E traverse.* Indeed, generally the stages are unevenly balanced from E to W and no ski runs are found to compare to those from the Col de Sonadon (Mont Durand glacier) and Col de Valpelline. * Now much reduced by Bouquetins biv.(p.57).

Saas Fee and Zermatt guides might disagree, but then they usually choose alternative routes to reduce the difficulties and improve the skiing—see HLR East to West notes at the end of

Part III. Finally, it is clearly advantageous to reach the Zermatt and Saas Fee areas with maximum fitness if planning to climb any major peaks.

STAGE 1: ARGENTIÈRE - ARGENTIÈRE HUT

Nowadays a very short stage due to the Grands Montets cableway. The construction of this lift has made it possible to bypass the Argentière hut, which in any case involves a detour, and to head straight for the Trient hut (see Route 14). Spending the night there guarantees better snow conditions for the descent to Champex the next day. However, especially from late April onwards, warmer weather can mean that the start from the Grands Montets top station will be made too late to ensure safe snow conditions for the crossing of the Col du Chardonnet. Therefore the traditional first stage to the Argentière hut (2771m.) is retained despite its brevity. Only fanatical purists or impecunious parties will wish to undertake the strenuous ascent from Argentière beside the piste to join the route described below at c.2620m. on the Argentière glacier! Some parties do start out from the intermediate station at the Croix de Lognan (1975m.).

The valley station of the Grands Montets lift (1240m.) lies 500m. S of Argentière (1257m.) on a slip road that branches off NE by Les Chosalets where the main road makes a right-angled bend at the bridge over the River Arve. A special bus service operates regularly from Chamonix.

11   (a) Take the cable car via the Croix de Lognan to the Grands Montets upper terminus, sited c.20m. below the summit of the Aiguille des Grands Montets (3297m.). Superb close-up view of the Aig. du Dru and Aig. Verte to the S with Mont Blanc filling in the background. To the ENE study the first part of Stage 2 up to the Col du Chardonnet.

Descend the made path to the Col des Grands Montets (3233m.) and ski E down the Rognons glacier (crevasses) on to the Argentière glacier at c.2620m. The main piste soon breaks off L(ENE). The Argentière glacier basin is walled by an unrivalled set of majestic ice faces. Cross the glacier E to the

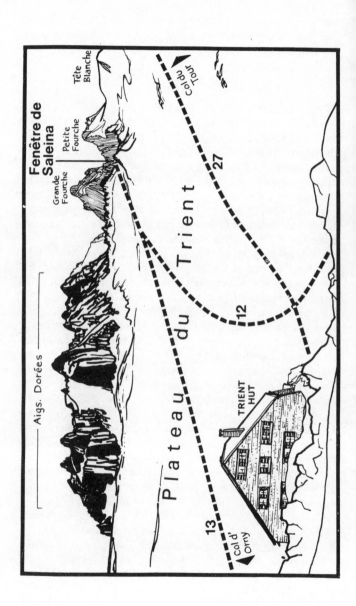

R(E) bank moraine and the Argentière hut 50m. above (1½ h.).

(b) From Argentière railway station walk 250m. N up the main road, turn R, cross the River Arve, go through the village and under the railway line. Turn R again and start S up the marked piste, veering SE towards the L(W) bank moraine of the Argentière glacier. At c.1500m. this route links up with the piste to Les Chosalets and the valley station of the cableway. Keep near the moraine, then curve SW up steep wooded slopes to the intermediate cableway station at the Croix de Lognan, restaurant (2 h.).

The piste now makes a gently rising traverse E to pass S of the closed Lognan hotel (now a military establishment) and leads SE up a basin to the L lateral moraine of the Argentière glacier. Go on to the glacier by pt.2338m. above an icefall and ascend its L bank with a narrow passage E of the Moraine des Rognons (LK 25, highest point indicated by pt.2754m. on LK 50) to join (a) at c.2620m. (3 h. to the hut, 5 h. from Argentière).

STAGE 2: ARGENTIÈRE HUT - COL DU CHARDONNET-FENÊTRE DE SALEINA - FENÊTRE DU CHAMOIS CHAMPEX

Together with Stage 4 this is the most serious part of the HLR and is subject to variable conditions. If surprised by bad weather between the Col du Chardonnet and the Fenêtre de Saleina, one must not attempt the very dangerous direct descent to Praz de Fort in the Val Ferret. In poor visibility finding the Fenêtre du Chamois creates a major problem and the descent from it requires the use of rope and crampons. Subsequently the delightful Arpette valley gives a splendid ski run provided that the snow has not softened too much. Outstanding scenery, particularly the view from the Col du Chardonnet.

12   Ski back down to the R(E) bank of the Argentière glacier and follow it NW to c.2600m. at the foot of the SW ridge of the Aig. d'Argentière W summit. Then head NE (loose rock ribs sometimes protrude) up on to the L(E) bank of the Chardonnet glacier. Work gradually L in the same direction up steep

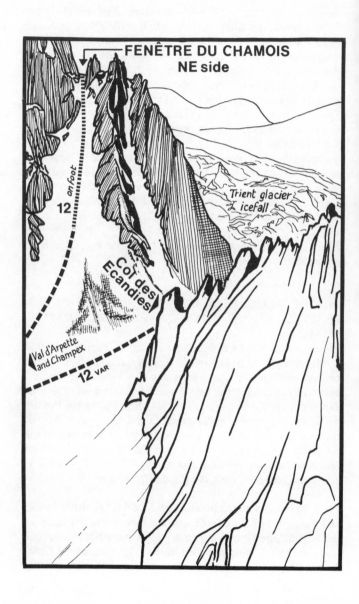

FENÊTRE DU CHAMOIS
NE side

on foot

12

Trient glacier
icefall

Col des
Ecandies

Val d'Arpette
and Champex

12 VAR

slopes to the middle of the glacier and the branch leading up to the Col du Chardonnet (3323m.). On the steepest part, an enclosed slope, it may be best to carry skis according to the snow conditions. Keep to the centre of the glacier on the straightforward upper slopes to reach the col (2½-3 h.).

A steep slope, about 45°, leads NE down on to the Saleina glacier 80m. below. It may be icy and should almost always be descended on foot wearing crampons. In dry conditions suitable rocks draped with old slings form habitual abseil points. Even in winter the bergschrund at the bottom often remains open. Now ski NE across the glacier to pt.3091m. at the foot of the rock rib coming down SE from the Grande Fourche, then head N into the basin between the Petite Fourche and the Aiguilles Dorées. Climb a steep slope on foot but without any difficulty to the Fenêtre de Saleina (3261m.) (1½ h.).

Go a few m. N on to the Trient glacier and at first ski NE below the Aiguilles Dorées over the Plateau du Trient towards the Trient hut, situated on the R bank, below and SSE of the Pointe d'Orny. Later head N down the R bank of the glacier to a prominent shoulder, marked by a cairn, W of the Petite Pointe d'Orny and level with the top of the icefall on the L. Now traverse a steep slope R and slightly downwards to the Fenêtre du Chamois (2985m.), a narrow rock gap S of the Col des Ecandies on the NW ridge of the Petite Pointe d'Orny. In good snow conditions ski across this slope, otherwise cross it on foot (1 h.). The Fenêtre du Chamois and its spot height are marked neither on the LK 50 nor LK 25.

On the N side of the gap a steep couloir drops 150m. to the head of the Arpette valley. Its snowy rocks are frequently verglassed and the top part may consequently be quite awkward. Rope up and wear crampons. Alternatively, in very bad conditions abseil (suitable rock spikes available). From 100m. below the gap it is normally possible to ski down the much wider lower part of the couloir to draw level with (E of) the Col des Ecandies (½-1 h.).

N.B. Given sufficient snow and safe conditions the Fenêtre du Chamois can be avoided by skiing down steeply R of the Trient glacier icefall from the shoulder W· of the Petite Pointe d'Orny and then ascending 50m. E to the Col des Ecandies

(2796m.). Rejoin the main route on the easy E side of the col. When practicable this pleasant variant gives more skiing and saves time.

Now ski down the upper basin of the Arpette valley, passing R of pt.2364m. Keep to the slopes on the R(E) side of the valley to reach the Arpette chalets (1627m.). Continue ENE through woods, later E after joining a piste, and pass the bottom station of the Breya chair lift (1498m.) before coming into Champex (1466m.) (1-2 h., 6½-8½ h. from the Argentière hut).

Stage 2 Variant: Descent via the Orny hut to Orsières
From the Plateau du Trient a descent ENE to Orsières (901m.) is actually easier than crossing the Fenêtre du Chamois. However, the Combe d'Orny is exposed to avalanches and lower down there is rarely enough snow for skiing.

13   Follow Route 12 to the Plateau du Trient (4-5 h.) and continue NE to the Col d'Orny (3098m.). Ski down the L bank of the Orny glacier and then its L lateral moraine to the Orny hut (2826m.) (½ h.). Now do not go E directly towards the Combe d'Orny on the summer route to La Breya and Orsières. Instead keep briefly to the glacier's L-hand moraine which curves SE. (The summer way down to Praz de Fort breaks off here and can be descended, but steep avalanche prone slopes on the S side of the Pointes des Chevrettes make this inadvisable.) Leave the moraine and head E to a gap between pt.2630m. and the Pointes des Chevrettes. Ski steeply E to the Lui des Revers slopes L(N) of pt.2274m. and NE into the Combe d'Orny valley basin by the Darbellay stream. A marked path descends wooded slopes on the L bank of the stream (at pt.1490m. a path forks off L to Champex), then crosses NE downwards past pt.1319m to Prassurny (1317m.), a hamlet just off the Orsières-Champex road (1½-2½ h., 6-8 h. from the Argentière hut).

Stages 1 and 2 Alternative Combination: Via the Trient hut
As noted above in the introduction to Stage 1, the Argentière-Champex section of the HLR across the N part of the Mont Blanc Range can be divided so as to stay overnight at the Trient hut instead of the Argentière hut. In this case it is essential to

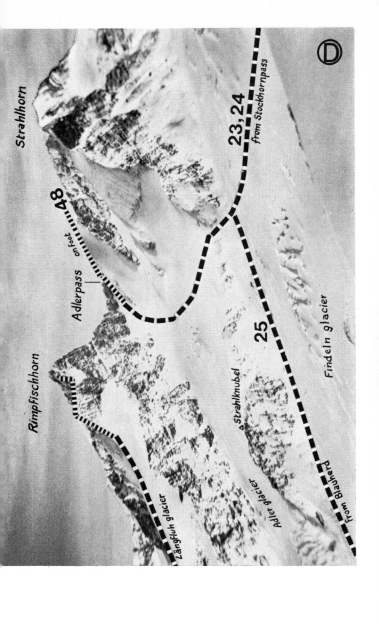

Strahlhorn

48
on foot

23, 24
from Stockhornpass

Adlerpass

Rimpfischhorn

25

△Strahlknubel

Findeln glacier

Längfluh glacier

Adler glacier

from Blauherd

Ⓓ

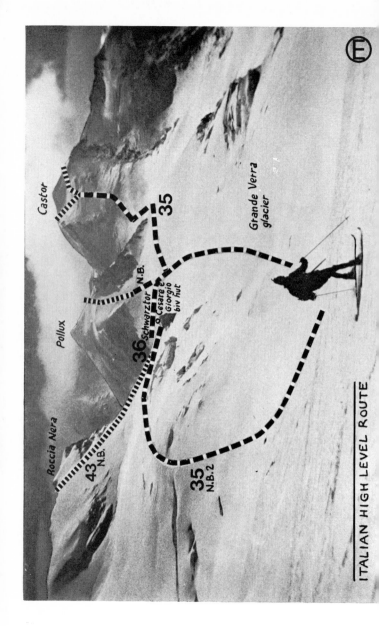

Castor

Pollux

Roccia Nera

Grande Verra glacier

35

N.B.

36 Schwarztor

35
N.B.2

43
N.B.

Q. Cesare e
Giorgio
biv hut

ITALIAN HIGH LEVEL ROUTE

Ⓔ

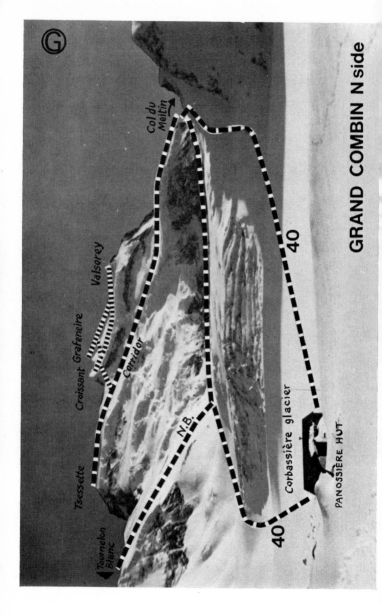

G

Tournelon Blanc

Tsessette

Croissant Grafeneire

Valsorey

Col du Meitin

Corridor

N.B.

Corbassière glacier

40

40

PANOSSIÈRE HUT

GRAND COMBIN N side

MONTE ROSA NW

take the earliest cable car up to the Grands Montets. Reaching the Trient hut on the first day ensures better snow conditions for the descent to Champex. The main disadvantage lies in the risk of bad weather coming on overnight: all routes from the Trient hut are dangerous (avalanches) after heavy snowfall and orientation in mist presents serious difficulties on the Plateau du Trient. Occasionally very fit parties complete Stages 1 and 2 in a day (8-9 h. at least), an idea only to be sensibly entertained if training ski tours have been undertaken beforehand.

14 Argentière-Trient hut. Reach c.2620m. on the Argentière glacier by Route 11(a) and cross it horizontally NE to the foot of the SW ridge of the Aig. d'Argentière W summit ($\frac{3}{4}$ h.). Now follow Route 12 to the Plateau du Trient. Ski to the Col d'Orny (3098m.) and ascend N to reach the Trient hut (3170m.) from the WNW by the L-hand curve (5 h. from the Grands Montets).

15 Trient hut-Champex. From the hut ski WNW on the gentle upper slopes of the Trient glacier to rejoin Route 12 W of the Pointe d'Orny (3-4 h. to Champex).

CHAMPEX - BOURG ST. PIERRE
Take the bus (infrequent service) to Orsières (901m.) in the Entremont valley. Change here and travel SSE (more regular bus service) up the Great St. Bernard road to Bourg St. Pierre (1632m.). 24 km. altogether.
N.B. See Routes 28 and 29 for a way of bridging the gap between the Mont Blanc Range and Pennine Alps without using roads.

STAGE 3: BOURG ST. PIERRE - VALSOREY HUT
An early start should be made as the slopes below the hut become avalanche prone after midday in certain conditions. Laden with four days provisions for the main section of the HLR to Zermatt this stage is physically demanding.

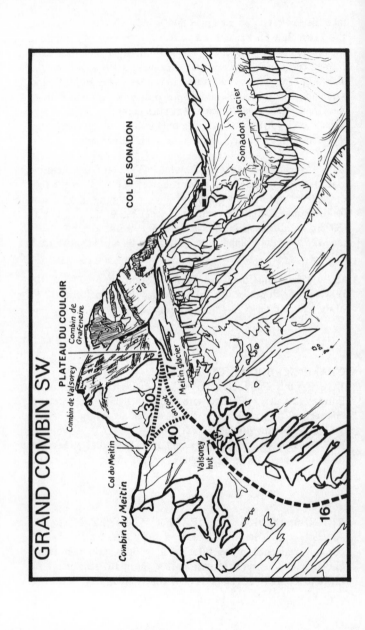

GRAND COMBIN SW

PLATEAU DU COULOIR

Combin de Valsorey

Combin de Grafeneire

Col du Meitin

Combin du Meitin

Meitin glacier

30

17

40 on foot

Valsorey hut

16

COL DE SONADON

Sonadon glacier

16   Leave the main road at the top (S) end of Bourg St. Pierre (signpost to Valsorey and Vélan huts) and cross fields SE into the Valsorey valley. Continue in the same direction on the R(N) bank of the stream, passing just above the Cordonna huts, at an easy angle to the Chalet d'Amont (2198m.) (2-2½ h.). From early April onwards the summer track will thus far often be largely clear of snow. Do not, however, go any farther on this path towards the rock barrier at pt.2352.5m. even if it is visible. Keep to the level valley bed and reach pt.2238m. Now head E through a narrow rock gorge to the former junction of the Tseudet and Valsorey glaciers. Follow the R-hand moraine of the Valsorey glacier briefly, then bear L(N) over the open slopes of the Grand Plan past pt.2606m. (2614m. on LK 25) to the 400m. high steep slope below the Botseresse and on the L of the rock spur that comes down from the Valsorey hut (3030m.). Climb the slope, trending NE higher up, by a series of zigzags and cross rocks R to the hut. In unsure snow conditions move diagonally R off the upper section of the slope to join the W edge of the broad rock spur and scramble up it to the hut (3 h., 5-5½ h. altogether).

STAGE 4: VALSOREY HUT - PLATEAU DU COULOIR COL DE SONADON - CHANRION HUT
The key passage on the HLR with unusual difficulties *by normal ski touring standards*. In good conditions the 600m. climb from the Valsorey hut to the Plateau du Couloir presents no particular problems to a competent ski mountaineer and its considerable reputation then seems greatly exaggerated. However, sometimes a large cornice defends the exit on to the Plateau du Couloir and the final slope is often ice—crampons are usually essential to save cutting steps and ice pegs or screws are occasionally needed. After heavy snowfall the avalanche risk must not be underestimated. The magnificent ski descent of the Mont Durand glacier is a highlight of the HLR, but in poor visibility complex route finding difficulties arise.

17   From the Valsorey hut the slope up to the Plateau du Couloir appears deceptively foreshortened. For the first 250/

300m. vertical interval it is possible to wear skis, but most parties prefer to climb on foot all the way. Ascend NE towards the Grand Combin de Valsorey over the Meitin glacier. Higher up the slope steepens to 45°. Once below the Col du Meitin slant progressively R(ESE) to reach the Plateau du Couloir 150-200m. L(N) of pt.3661m. according to the prevailing conditions. The final slope, where a few broken rocks may protrude, is quite exposed: if the exit is not corniced, there will almost invariably be some ice (2-2½ h.). Should the cornice assume abnormal proportions, one can head for the point where it merges with the rocks of the Combin de Valsorey.

The Plateau du Couloir is a flat glacier terrace immediately below the S face of the Combin de Valsorey. Cross it SE and go down a short steep slope (often on foot) ESE on to the upper névés of the Sonadon glacier which is traversed SE towards the Col de Sonadon (3504m.). Rise slightly to the col which is situated at the foot of the Grand Combin de Grafeneire S ridge (1 h.).

Now ski briefly SE down the Mont Durand glacier. Soon trend R (SSE) to the R bank of the glacier by the Grande Tête de By and thus avoid the large icefall that stretches across the centre of the glacier at c.3200m. Because of this icefall one must not attempt to descend directly E from the Col de Sonadon. Keep to the R bank over the N slopes of the Tête Blanche de By to reach a large glacier basin. Continue E down the R bank of the glacier to c.2700m. The descent does not however follow the Mont Durand glacier to the valley below. Instead, a slightly rising traverse ENE along a broad terrace leads to pt.2735.7m. (trig. marker), a shoulder on the long NE ridge of Mont Avril.

Ski SE on to the tongue of the Fenêtre glacier (pt.2559m.) and continue NNE down steeper open slopes, finishing in the Grande Chermotane valley basin E of pt.2206m. (1½-2 h. from Col de Sonadon).

The rock gorge on the R provides the access to the Otemma glacier: see Stage 5, Route 18. Cross the Otemma stream and ascend gentle slopes NNW, passing E of La Paume (chalet), to the Chanrion hut (2460m.) on a small plateau (¾ h., 5¼-6¼ h. altogether).

STAGE 5: CHANRION HUT - VIGNETTES HUT

The ascent of the 10 km. long Otemma glacier forms the most monotonous part of the HLR notwithstanding the splendid scenery. To save a day strong parties sometimes combine Stages 4 and 5, and in that case omit the Chanrion hut by making straight for the Otemma glacier from the Grande Chermotane valley basin (9-10 h. from the Valsorey to the Vignettes hut)·

By using the new Singla bivouac hut (3180m.), sited well above the L bank of the Otemma glacier, one can bypass both the Chanrion and Vignettes huts while also saving a day. From c.2900m. on the Otemma glacier (combine Routes 17 and 18 thus far) climb SE up the E side of the Blanchen glacier (unnamed on LK 50, forms the basin headed by Le Blanchen to the SE) to c.3075m. and slant SW up to the biv. hut on the S ridge of the Aiguillette rock island (3198.7m., named on LK 25 only) (1 h., 8½-9 h. from Valsorey hut, 7½-11 h. to Zermatt via the Col du Petit Mont Collon variant mentioned in the introduction to Stage 6).

The traverse of the Pigne d'Arolla forms a more enterprising connection between the Chanrion and Vignettes huts and offers an interesting alternative to this stage, see Route 19.

18   From the Chanrion hut ski back down the gentle slopes SSE to the head of the Grande Chermotane valley basin. A rock gorge, formed by the Otemma stream, leads SE to the moraines of the Otemma glacier. Now bear NE round the S spur of the Pointe d'Otemma on to the glacier.

Note that both of the more direct summer routes from the hut across steep slopes to the Otemma glacier at c.2600m. and c.2520m. respectively are exceedingly dangerous due to avalanches in winter/spring. On the other hand it is possible to pass R(S) of pt.2405m. (a small knoll) above the rock gorge by a vaguely defined band and to then trend NE on to the Otemma glacier.

Keep to the centre of the gently angled glacier, heading NE in the direction of the Petit Mont Collon which divides the glacier into a N and S branch. Opposite the foot of the NW ridge of La Singla at c.2920m. bear NNE over the L-hand (N) branch towards the broad saddle of the Col de Chermotane

(3067m.). Leave the lowest point just to the R and, slanting slightly L, continue N to reach a shoulder (immediately L of pt.3162m. on LK 25) by a very short steep slope. Now traverse the glacier terrace at the foot of the E slopes of the Pigne d'Arolla horizontally N to the Col des Vignettes and go R(E) for a few min. along a short ridge to the Vignettes hut (3157m.) (4½-5 h.). In mist and without a track the hut is difficult to find: take particular care not to miss the abovementioned shoulder as a traverse R below it only leads on to the impassable Vuibe glacier.

Stage 5 Variant: Chanrion hut-Pigne d'Arolla-Vignettes hut
A splendid traverse, but more strenuous than the normal way to the Vignettes hut and consequently rather neglected, especially in this direction. It deserves more attention. Extremely few mountains of comparative height in the Alps can be climbed to the top on skis from two sides.

19   From the Chanrion hut head N below the W ridge of the Pointe d'Otemma and NE past pt.2622m. over the L(E) lateral moraine on to the Breney glacier. Ascend it, keeping R of the central moraine, towards pt.2955m. where the Serpentine and Breney glaciers merge. Continue NE and climb a steep broad couloir on foot between the Serpentine rocks on the L and the icefall on the R to reach the gentler upper slopes which lead NNE up the basin between the rock islet at pt.3434m. and the Pointes de Breney to the plateau depression of the Col de Breney (3639m.) (4½-5 h.).
    N.B. A longer option lies up the Serpentine glacier to the Col de la Serpentine (3547m.), then E to a steep slope (the Mur de la Serpentine, often icy) SW of pt.3592m. and NE to the Col de Breney (about 5 h.).
    Ascend easy slopes ENE to the saddle (c.3740m.) between the Pigne d'Arolla (3796m.) and pt. 3772m. and go N to the top (½ h., 5-5½ h. from the Chanrion hut).
    Return to the saddle immediately S of the summit and ski down pleasant open slopes E to c.3350m. In good conditions continue steeply and directly down to the glacier terrace at the foot of the E slopes, and traverse horizontally N to the Col des

Vignettes. Finally go R up a short ridge to the Vignettes hut ($\frac{3}{4}$ h., $5\frac{3}{4}$-$6\frac{1}{2}$ h. altogether).

In unfavourable conditions (hard snow/ice or limited visibility) ski SE from c.3400m. towards the Col de Chermotane to pass between the rocks at pt.3189.4m. to the R and the shoulder crossed by Route 18 to the L. At c.3100m. cross NE up to the shoulder and so reach the glacier terrace as above ($\frac{1}{2}$ h. longer).

STAGE 6: VIGNETTES HUT - COL DE L'EVÊQUE - COL DU MONT BRULÉ - COL DE VALPELLINE - ZERMATT
By far the longest stage in distance on the HLR with a considerable amount of downhill skiing. A magnificent traverse of three passes amidst quite outstanding scenery. It should only be undertaken in settled weather because the orientation is otherwise complex. In poor visibility the Col du Mont Brulé, which provides the sole passage between the Upper Arolla and Upper Tsa de Tsan glaciers, is especially hard to locate and the huge crevasse zones on the Stockji glacier become treacherous. If surprised by bad weather this traverse can be abandoned between the Col de l'Evêque and the Col du Mont Brulé by descending the Upper and Lower Arolla glaciers NW to Arolla.

However, the new Bouquetins biv. hut noted on p.57 completely changes the serious aspect of this stage, which can now be broken into two unequal parts by stopping overnight at the biv. hut. It lies only 15 min. away horizontally N across the entrance to the big gl. bay under the Col du Mont Brulé.

It is a rare occurrence for a party to go from the Chanrion hut to Zermatt in a day, but in this event head ENE from c.2920m. on the Otemma glacier (Route 18) up its S branch towards the Col du Petit Mont Collon (3292m.). Pass S above the col and continue E across the upper slopes of the Mont Collon glacier to join the route below at the Col de l'Evêque (10-14 h. from the Chanrion hut to Zermatt, about 40 km.).

20 From the Vignettes hut return by the short ridge to the Col des Vignettes and traverse the glacier terrace below the E slopes of the Pigne d'Arolla horizontally to a shoulder before skiing down steeply but briefly towards the Col de Chermotane. Now cross the large glacier plateau SSE to pass L(E) of its lowest point and ascend the Mont Collon glacier SE, leaving the Petit Mont Collon to the R, towards the Col de l'Evêque (3392m.), the second gap SW of l'Evêque and not the snow saddle (pt.3399m.) at the foot of the SW ridge proper of l'Evêque. Finally curve L(E) up to the col which is sometimes slightly corniced (2 h.).

Ski down steep glacier slopes E towards the Col Collon (3117m.), turning a crevasse zone R. Near the col head down NNE below the NW face of La Vierge, a big rock island, on to the upper plateau of the Upper Arolla glacier at c.2900m. and go E towards the Col du Mont Brulé (3213m.). Take care not to confuse this col with the Col de Tsa de Tsan which lies ¾ km. further S and nearer Mont Brulé. The Col du Mont Brulé is the central gap on the rock ridge bordering the Upper Arolla glacier to the E. Rather than making directly for the col, keep slightly S so as to curve back up to the final 100m. steep snow slope which is usually climbed on foot. Avalanche danger after heavy snowfall (1½-2 h.).

The next stretch between the Col du Mont Brulé and the Col de Valpelline (3568m.) forms the only part of the classic HLR on Italian terrain. Ski down on to the isolated basin of the Upper Tsa de Tsan glacier and head along the E base of the Bouquetins towards the icefall below and S of the Col des Bouquetins. Keep as high as possible on account of the tremendous icefall to the R. Ascend ENE below the S face of the Tête Blanche to the Col de Valpelline, finishing up a steeper slope (1½-2 h.).

From the col the Tête Blanche or Tête de Valpelline can be climbed easily in ¾ h. and both summits are superb viewpoints, particularly of the Dent d'Hérens and Matterhorn which are now first seen at close quarters.

In good conditions the following descent of the Stockji and Tiefmatten glaciers gives an outstanding ski run, but great care must be exercised on account of the numerous crevasses. Ski NE towards the S limits of the Wandfluh rocks, avoiding crevasse zones L(W). At c.3200m. head R(SSE) away from the Stockji rock island and down a steep slope, sometimes strewn with sérac debris, on to the Tiefmatten glacier. At c.2980m. bear ENE along the glacier's L(N) edge to pass between the Stockji and pt.2805m. but much nearer the former. (It is also possible to ski to pt.3041m. on the Stockji before going down steeply S towards pt.2805m. to rejoin the usual route.) This steep basin leads to the head of the Zmutt glacier near pt.2631m. at the E foot of the Stockji (1-1½ h.).

From this point the Schönbiel hut (2694m.) can be seen above the moraine on the L(N) bank of the Zmutt glacier. Anyone wishing to avoid a descent to the valley (Zermatt) and preferring to follow the alternative way to the Monte Rosa hut, detailed under Route 22, must now cross the glacier NNE and climb the moraines well to the L of the hut, followed by a lightly descending traverse to it (½ h., 6½-8 h. from the Vignettes hut).

For Zermatt ski E down the Zmutt glacier, at first keeping nearer its L(N) bank. Once the snow begins to melt, scree and large rocks make this run unpleasant. Continue in the same direction to Stafelalp (2199m.). The hotel there is now open.
Ski ENE through the woods to soon join the marked piste (Weisse Perle run) from Schwarzsee. It leads above the R(S) bank of the Zmutt stream almost to Furi (1886m.), then L(NE) over meadows through Blatten hamlet to finish at the S end of Zermatt (1614m.) next to the customs house by the bridge below the cable car station. Officially it is forbidden to ski along the Zmutt-Zermatt path above the L(W) bank of the stream; this is reserved for walkers (1½-3 h. depending upon the snow conditions, 7½-10½ h. from the Vignettes hut).

N.B. After March insufficient snow generally makes the ski run from Furi-Zermatt impracticable. Skiers then take the cable car down. Indeed, once the snow line has risen above 2000m. in spring it becomes quicker to follow the jeep track from Stafelalp that passes along the S side of the reservoir to the barrage, then cross the dam wall L (pt.1972m. on LK 25) and walk down through Zmutt (1936m.) on the L bank of the river to Zermatt.

STAGE 7: ZERMATT - MONTE ROSA HUT
A short day assuming the use of mechanical aids. In winter/

spring a variety of ways can be taken to the Monte Rosa hut (2795m.), but the traditional route is described below.

Very briefly the other possibilities are: 1) Take the cable car to Trockener Steg, then the Gandegg and Theodulpass ski tows to 3294m. on the Upper Theodul glacier. Ski down the Lower Theodul glacier passing between pt.3201m. and pt.3032m. Later turn the icefall W on the L bank before crossing NE past pt.2536m. on to the Gorner glacier—see Route 22 (2-2½ h. from Theodulpass). 2) Take the Gornergrat railway to its upper terminus and the Stockhorn cable car to pt.3403m. Pass immediately N of the Stockhorn summit to reach the Stockhorn-pass (3398m.), a mere saddle, and ski SW over the Gorner glacier to pt.2965m. at the top of the lateral moraine. Go down W on the L of the moraine crest to the Gorner lakes (2650m.) and ascend SSW to join the usual approach (2½ h. from the Stockhorn cableway terminus). In the context of the HLR this approach is rather pointless as one would then do better to go directly to the Britannia hut by Route 24. 3) Follow the jeep road from Furi towards the Boden glacier snout and go up this to the S foot of the Rifelhorn by pt.2488m., then over the Gorner glacier (5-5½ h.). Adequate snow on the glacier snout is essential. A tiresome approach.

The circuitous line of the classic HLR between Zermatt and Saas Fee results from the modern tendency, due to lift and piste developments, to reject the once popular ski route across the Theodul glacier that enables the tourer to avoid Zermatt and go directly from the Schönbiel hut to the Monte Rosa hut; see Route 22. Yet the wish to climb the Dufourspitze or the Signalkuppe dissuades most parties from omitting the Monte Rosa hut by going directly to Saas Fee; see Routes 24 and 25.

21　　Travel by the Gornergrat railway (50 per cent reduction with a Swiss Holiday Ticket) via Rifelalp and Rifelberg to Rotenboden station (2819m.), the last stop before the upper terminus. The journey takes approx. 40 min. The hut remains in view almost all the way from Rotenboden.

Descend S to pt.2775m. in a slight dip. Go 400m. horizontally ESE and then SW down a steep slope E of the Moritzloch couloir (unmarked on LK 50, Murischloch on LK 25) to reach the Gorner glacier c.200m. E of pt.2564m. A direct descent of the Moritzloch couloir to pt.2564m. is often unpleasant. At first head ESE up the glacier, moving towards the central moraine.

N.B. Once the S side of the Gornergrat is fairly free of snow (probably by mid-May) it is quicker to follow the summer track from pt.2775m. on a long descending traverse (avalanche debris) past pt.2678m. down to the Gorner glacier at c.2640m. Do not attempt this line in doubtful snow conditions when there may be serious avalanche danger.

Go SE on to the Grenz glacier and ascend this in the same direction to the height of the hut before crossing horizontally L(NE) between large crevasses and finally over the moraine crest to it (2 h.).

Unless there is very little snow do not use the summer route which leaves the glacier NW of the hut and leads to it by a path up slabby rocks and the moraine ridge.

Stages 6 and 7 Variant: Schönbiel hut-Hörnli ski lift-Theodul glacier-Monte Rosa hut
Taking this route enables Saas Fee to be reached from Bourg St. Pierre without a valley stop. The line described here was long accepted as the best way from the Zmutt glacier (Schönbiel hut) to the Monte Rosa hut, but this leg of the journey across the skiing areas of Zermatt seems to have lost any modern day purpose due to the proliferation of cableways and ski tows; yet probably only the tourer has time to appreciate fully the splendour of his surroundings.

The way off to the Schönbiel hut is detailed under Route 20 (Stage 6).

22   From the Schönbiel hut head briefly W before skiing down SW on to the Schönbiel glacier which flows into the Zmutt glacier. Avalanché danger often renders the more direct descent E and SE on to the glacier inadvisable. Now descend E as by Route 20 towards Stafelalp. Pass S of the café/ hotel c.100m. higher up and make a rising traverse ESE across the Obere

Stafelalp slopes to join the Hörnli ski lift piste (Front run on the W side of the tow) at c.2420m. Ascend it N to the top station (2775m.) and continue SW on to the Furgg glacier below the E face of the Matterhorn. Gradually curve SE and go up the gentle slopes of the Upper Theodul glacier, crossing the Furggsattel ski lift and passing the bottom of the Theodulpass ski lift, until S of pt.3201m. (5½ h.). N.B. The Theodul hut, immediately N above the Theodulpass, can be reached in ½ h. by going S below the E slopes of the Theodulhorn.

Now ski down E on to the Lower Theodul glacier between pt.3201m. and pt.3032m., turning crevasses R. Then head N towards pt.2881m. on the L bank to turn the icefall W before crossing NE over to the R bank. This section coincides with the popular off-piste ski run from the Furggsattel via the Gorner glacier to Furi. Pass pt.2536m. at the N foot of the Triftji to reach the L bank of the Gorner glacier. Work towards its centre and go ESE over the gently inclined glacier to join Route 21 coming up from Rotenboden (2-2½ h. to the Monte Rosa hut from the Theodulpass ski lift, 7½-8 h. from the Schönbiel hut).

N.B. The use of mechanical aids shortens this stage appreciably and also adds to the downhill skiing. Two combinations are suggested. The more complex option (ii) retains a far greater Alpine flavour.

(i) Descend from the Schönbiel hut to Furi as by Route 20 (1-2 h.). Take the cable car via Furgg to Trockener Steg, then the Gandegg and Theodulpass ski tows to pt.3294m. on the Upper Theodul glacier (¾ h.). Ski down NE towards pt.3201m. to join Route 22 (2-2½ h. to the hut, 3¾ h.-5¼ h. altogether).

(ii) Follow Route 22 to the Obere Stafelalp but cross E to the bottom station of the Hörnli ski lift (2330m.), c.350m. E of pt.2361.7m. Take the lift to the top station (2775m.). Go SW to pass R(W) of pt.2785m. and make a semi-circular curve (unmarked piste) before skiing NE past pt. 2549m. and along an enclosed little valley to Furgg (2432m.) (½ h.). Continue as by (a) (5-5½ h. altogether). This option can be simplified by ascending the Weisse Perle piste from the Hörnli ski lift to Schwarzsee (2582m.) (restaurant and dormitory) and then taking the cableway link down to Furgg.

STAGE 8: MONTE ROSA HUT - STOCKHORNPASS -
ADLERPASS - BRITANNIA HUT

The highest pass on the classic HLR, the Adlerpass (3802m.), is
crossed during this long stage. From the pass the Strahlhorn is
a rewarding addition (1-1½ h.) and a comparatively easy 4000m.
peak (see Route 48). Snow conditions vary considerably on the
W side of the Adlerpass. If no mountains are to be climbed
from the Britannia hut, then the short final stage of the HLR
down to Saas Fee can obviously be completed the same day.

23　　From the Monte Rosa hut there are two roundabout
ways of reaching the upper end of the Gorner glacier L(S) bank
moraine near pt.2965m. Due to steep rocks and the lower
icefall of the Monte Rosa glacier one cannot cross directly NE
to this point. Option (a) is quickest providing the correct line
is taken.

(a)　Ascend SE as for the Monte Rosa summits, keeping
L(E) of the Grenz glacier R lateral moraine crest, to a prominent
large rock below the two rock arms coming down from the
Ober Plattje (incorrectly placed on LK 50) at c.3000m. near
pt.3012m. Now go L(N) across the Monte Rosa glacier, losing
a little height, towards a long broken rock rib coming down
from pt.3263.9m. This rib divides the Monte Rosa glacier from
the Gorner glacier. Climb up to it at c.3050m. and, depending
upon the snow conditions, normally scramble over loose rocks
up the final bit to the ridge. Cross horizontally or slightly
downwards NE on to the Gorner glacier above the upper end
of the L(S) bank moraine (1½ h.).

(b)　Cross the R lateral moraine SW on to the Grenz glacier
and continue horizontally between large crevasses before skiing
N down to the Gorner lakes (2650m.) and the bottom of the
L(S) bank moraine of the Gorner glacier. Ascend quite steeply
R(S) of the moraine crest past pt.2965m. on to the glacier
(1½-2 h.).

Now ascend gently NE across the glacier to the Stockhornpass
(3394m., variable on　LK 50), a poorly defined flat saddle at
the foot of the broad E ridge of the Stockhorn (1½ h.).

Ski NNE on to the Findeln glacier with numerous crevasses
down to c.3140m. and cross it N towards the opening between

the Strahlknubel rocks and the WSW ridge of the Adlerhorn. Keeping nearer the latter, climb the short steep slope up to the Adler glacier and head NNE across the large glacier basin towards the S foot of the Rimpfischhorn. Trend NE to the foot of the steep snow/ice slope below the Adlerpass (3802m.). Slant up it from L to R (bergschrund) beside the Rimpfischhorn rocks, often making use of a snow gully immediately R of the rocks, on foot to the col (3 h., 6-6½ h. from the hut). Avoid the open slope on the R which is prone to slab avalanches or otherwise frequently ice.

Ski NNE down the Allalin glacier, keeping L at first below the E face of the Rimpfischhorn. At c.3450m., however, turn a crevasse zone well to the R(E) and continue down gentler slopes below the ENE ridge of the Allalinhorn. Veer E to ski round the rock islet pt.3143.3m. on its R(E) side, then cross the Hohlaub glacier horizontally NNE to the foot of the Hinter Allalin. Climb a short steep slope NE to the Britannia hut (3029m.) (1-1½ h., 7-8 h. altogether).

Stages 7 and 8 Variant: Zermatt-Adlerpass-Britannia hut
A day can be saved by omitting the Monte Rosa hut and going straight from Zermatt to the Britannia hut, arguably the logical choice in the sole context of the HLR. This, however, means sacrificing the opportunity to climb one of the Monte Rosa summits, something that should not be missed if sufficient time is available and the conditions are suitable. Two ways are possible and both use uphill transport at the start. Route 24 is slightly shorter and the normal choice. Route 25 is rarely taken yet much cheaper.

24   From Zermatt take the railway to the Gornergrat (3089m.). It is important to travel on the earliest train to have a chance of reasonable snow conditions later on. Continue by cable car via Hohtälli (3286m.) to the Stockhorn terminus at pt.3403m. Go past pt.3423m. along the snowy W ridge of the Stockhorn (3532m.). Pass a few m. L(N) of the summit and ski down the E ridge, turning pt.3462m. L(N), to the Stockhornpass (3398m.) where Route 23 is joined (1 h., 5-6 h. to the Britannia hut).

25   From Zermatt take the earliest trainlift to Sunnegga (2289m.) and the gondola cableway to Blauherd (2570m.). Traverse E past Stellisee to the Fluhalp hotel (2616m.) (possibly closed, ½ h.).   Continue E and cross the R bank moraine by pt.2697m. on to the Findeln glacier.   Work gradually towards the centre of the glacier to avoid crevasse zones and return to the R(N) bank at the confluence with the Adler glacier.   Head E below (S of) the Strahlknubel to join Route 23 at c.3180m. below the short steep slope up to the Adler glacier (2½ h. from Blauherd, 6-6½ h. to the Britannia hut).

STAGE 9: BRITANNIA HUT - EGGINERJOCH - SAAS FEE
A short final stage, consequently often preceded by or combined with the ascent of a mountain (see Routes 48-50 for possibilities). Given good snow conditions the ski descent from the Egginerjoch makes for an enjoyable conclusion to the HLR despite being a crowded piste in fine weather.   If insufficient snow remains to ski to Saas Fee, then the Felskinn cable car can be boarded at its middle station (c.2600m.).

26   From the Britannia hut cross the upper slopes of the Kessjen glacier NW to the Egginerjoch (2991m.) in ½ h. Ski NW down a cwm and soon join the marked Felskinn piste. Pass pt.2792m., keeping to the R(E) bank of the Fee glacier. Continue N down the moraines and the valley bed (minor variants possible) to Bifig and the valley terminus of the Felskinn cable car (1840m.), 15 min. SSW of Saas Fee (1790m.) which after the snow has melted is reached by an asphalt road through Kalbermatten (1¼-2 h. from the hut).

HLR EAST TO WEST
The majority of parties follow the HLR from W to E (see the introduction to Part III) and the tour is therefore described thus.   For those parties who nevertheless choose to journey from E to W a brief outline of the individual stages with some additional comments is given below.   Variants already described are not mentioned again.

Stage 1: *Saas Fee-Britannia hut*. See Route 10.

Stage 2: *Britannia hut-Monte Rosa hut*. Follow Route 48 for the Strahlhorn to the Adlerpass, then reverse Route 23. Note that with option (a) the descent of the rock rib dividing the Gorner glacier from the Monte Rosa glacier can be awkward. Descend the deceptive slope below the Adlerpass on foot.

Stage 3: *Monte Rosa hut-Zermatt*. Reverse Route 21 to join the piste at Rotenboden (2-2½ h.) or ski down the Gorner glacier to Furi provided there is plenty of snow.
If no ascents are planned from the Monte Rosa hut combine Stages 2 and 3 to go from the Britannia hut to Zermatt by reversing Route 23 as far as the Findeln glacier and then skiing down its L bank to join the piste near Grünsee (5-6 h. to Zermatt). Due to the Felskinn cable car it is now even possible to go straight from Saas Fee to Zermatt.

Stage 4: *Zermatt-Schönbiel hut*. See the last three paragraphs of Route 20 (4½ h.) and Schönbiel hut on p. 54.

Stage 5: *Schönbiel hut-Vignettes hut*. Reverse Route 20 (9-10 h.). It takes little longer to make directly for the Chanrion hut from the Col de l'Evêque, see the second paragraph of the introduction to Stage 6 (about 1-1½ h. extra). Bouquetins biv. overnight option.

Stage 6: *Vignettes hut-Chanrion hut*. Reverse Route 18 (2-3 h.). The Otemma glacier gives an extremely dull ski run. In this direction the variant by the Pigne d'Arolla (Routes 42 and 19) is therefore popular (4 h.), recommended.

Stage 7: *Chanrion hut-Valsorey hut-Bourg St. Pierre*. Reverse Routes 17 and 16 (9-12 h.). More serious than anything in the opposite direction and consequently often avoided. Some parties already abandon the classic HLR at the Vignettes hut, traverse the Pigne d'Arolla to the Dix hut, then the Rosablanche to the Mont Fort hut and Verbier. Recommended. Reverse Routes 32, 31 and 3.

Some skiers avoid the Plateau du Couloir by crossing from the Chanrion hut over the Fenêtre de Durand (2805m.) (start by reversing Route 17 to the Fenêtre glacier) via the Balme and Glacier chalets to Ollomont in Italy (4-5 h.), travel by road via Aosta to Courmayeur, take the cable car from La Palud to the Col du Géant and conclude the tour with the descent to Chamonix—a superb run down but hardly ski mountaineering.

A particularly ambitious variant crosses from the Plateau du Couloir (thus far by reversing Route 17) to the Col du Meitin and the Corbassière glacier (see Route 30). Go down to the Panossière hut (9-9½ h. from the Chanrion hut) or from pt.3155.5m. climb to the Col de Panossière (3458m.) and ski down the L bank of the Boveyre glacier, moving over to the R bank by pt. 2790m. Descend moraines SW, cross minor basins to pt.2204m. (chalet) and go down W past Creux du Max (1975m.) to the Great St. Bernard road between Liddes and Bourg St. Pierre (5 h. from Panossière hut, 11-12 h. directly from the Chanrion hut). Much finer downhill skiing than from the Valsorey hut to Bourg St. Pierre, none the less serious with avalanche danger at times.

Stage 8: Champex-Trient hut. Reverse Route 15 (6½ h.). Late in the season when the slopes on the N side of the Combe d'Orny are largely clear of snow the shortest access starts from the Grands Plans top station (2188m.) of the Breya chairlift. Follow the summer path which traverses steep slopes SW below the long rock ridge running WSW and rises W through a moraine valley to the Orny hut, then reverse Route 13 (4 h.).

Stage 9: Trient hut-Argentière. Reverse Route 14 to the Argentière glacier, then 11(b) on the Grands Montets-Argentière piste (5-5½ h.). One may follow either the L or R bank of the Chardonnet glacier but keep away from the ruptured centre below c.3150m. When sufficient snow remains on the lower slopes, the descent from the Col du Chardonnet to the valley gives the finest ski run on the classic HLR from E to W.

PART IV

ALTERNATIVE HIGH LEVEL ROUTES

Most of the itineraries described here are equally fine ski tours, generally following more roundabout routes or taking less frequented lines. While the very popular HLR from Verbier to Zermatt presents no mountaineering problem comparable with the Plateau du Couloir on the classic route, the Italian HLR is a more serious undertaking at a higher constant altitude and amidst remote surroundings. Some parties prefer to divide the central part of the HLR by descending to Arolla. Others choose to cover only a portion of the HLR, but in more detail by including some mtn. ascents. As with the classic HLR most of these tours are best taken from W to E and all are described thus to preserve the continuity.

HLR Extensions

The undermentioned possibility is very rarely carried out and requires excellent snow conditions, but very experienced and fit mountaineers can traverse Mont Blanc from the Grands Mulets hut (Routes 1 and 39) to the Col du Midi (see p. 107), then enjoy the famous Vallée Blanche ski run (see p. 108) (possibly sleeping at the Requin hut) and leave the Mer de Glace NE of the Montenvers to climb steeply to the Grands Montets at the start of the classic HLR.

At the other end of the route, eastwards from the Saas valley one can cross N or S of the Weissmies group to the Simplonpass. A traverse from the Almagell side valley via the Zwischbergenpass (3267m.) and the Weissmiessattel (3406m., spot height only on LK 50) to Simplon (1476m.) constitutes a very long and serious expedition (10-12 h.).* However, an easier and safer extension of the HLR is achieved by traversing the Simelipass (3023m.) and the Sirwoltensattel (2621m.) from Saas Balen or even the

Weissmies hut (see p. 132) to Niederalp (1815m.) on the S ramp
of the Simplonpass road (6½-8 h.). *But see also p. 132.

Le Tour-Albert Premier hut-Col du Tour-Fenêtre du Chamois-Champex

An alternative way of crossing the Mont Blanc Range to that
described in Stages 1 and 2 of the classic HLR (see Routes
11-15). Prior to the construction of the Grands Montets cable
lift this way was almost as popular, but it has since become
relatively neglected. The sole advantage of this route lies in a
shorter and less strenuous second day. While the scenery is
very fine, notably the views of the Aig. du Chardonnet, it cannot
compare with the tremendous faces surrounding the Argentière
glacier basin. Diagram, p. 60.

Reach the Albert Premier hut by Route 2.

27   From the Albert Premier hut cross to the Tour glacier
and ascend SE, usually passing S of the rock outcrop pt.2883m.
Continue over undulating slopes and pass the narrow glacier
bay leading up to the Col Supérieur du Tour (3288m.) on the
L. At c.3120m. bear E towards the Col du Tour (3281m.), the
gap immediately NW of the Tête Blanche. Climb a short broad
couloir on foot to the col (2 h.).

On the Swiss side of the pass ski ENE over the gently inclined
upper slopes of the Plateau du Trient to join Route 12 in a few
min. (2½-4 h. to Champex, 4½-6 h. altogether). N.B. To descend
via the Orny hut to Orsières continue skiing ENE over the
Plateau du Trient to the Col d'Orny where Route 13 is joined
(4-5½ h. from the Albert Premier hut to the Orsières-Champex
road).

Le Tour-Plateau du Trient by the Grands glacier

A little known and rarely taken line provides the quickest route
from the Chamonix valley to the Plateau du Trient. Aesthetically
it is not a satisfactory alternative to the classic HLR. From the
top station of the Col de Balme lift above Le Tour steep slopes
lead up to pt.2772m. on the N ridge of the Pointe des Berons
(de Bron). The small Berons glacier is crossed ESE to the
depression SSW of the Croix des Berons. A slanting ascent to

the SE of the Grands glacier, past the foot of the NW spur of the Aig. du Midi (des Grands), is then made to the col (c.3300m.) between the Aig. du Pissoir and Le Pissoir which gives access to the upper (W) slopes of the Plateau du Trient (3½-4 h.). For the continuation to Champex or Orsières join Route 12 or 13. For the Trient hut on the opposite (E) bank of the plateau ski to the Col d'Orny and ascend briefly N before reaching it by a L-hand curve.

Three Cols Traverse

After the HLR and Mont Blanc the celebrated Three Cols Traverse (Tour des Trois Cols) over five glaciers from the Argentière hut to the Albert Premier hut or vice versa forms the next most popular ski tour in the Mont Blanc Range. It leads via the Col du Chardonnet and the Fenêtre de Saleina to the Plateau du Trient as by Route 12, then across the Col du Tour by reversing Route 27 (5-6 h. from hut to hut).

Connection between the Mont Blanc Range and the Pennine Alps

Strictly speaking, due to the use of transport from Champex to Bourg St. Pierre, there remains a gap on the HLR. The area between the Swiss Val Ferret and the Val d'Entremont is omitted because the mtns. are low (under 3000m.), consequently sometimes devoid of snow by spring and in any case give undistinguished ski runs with avalanche dangers. The original summer version of the HLR crossed the Col des Planards from Ferret to Bourg St. Pierre. The two-day itinerary outlined briefly below will interest mainly those determined to avoid roads and is included partly for the sake of completeness. It should not be attempted immediately after a heavy snowfall or in soft snow conditions. Route 28 also forms an ambitious additional variant to Stage 2 of the classic HLR. The LK 25 map is useful for Route 29.

28 *Argentière hut-Col du Chardonnet-Col des Planereuses - A Neuve hut-La Fouly*

(a) Leave Route 12 from the Argentière hut on the Saleina glacier below the Col du Chardonnet. Descend the R bank of the glacier to c.2660m. and ascend E, later curving S up to the

Col des Planereuses (3030m.). Traverse the Planereuses glacier S, finishing up a short couloir to the Col Supérieur de Crête Sèche (3024 m., spot height only on map 400 m. W of the Col de Crête Sèche), and the Treutse Bô glacier SW up to the gap at pt.3113m. (Col Supérieur des Essettes, unnamed on map). Descend a steep gully SW on foot at first and then ski down SE to the A Neuve hut (2735m.) (7-7½ h. from the Argentière hut).

(b) Do not descend the summer route to La Fouly (1593m.). To ensure the safest snow conditions wait until late afternoon or if in doubt even early the following morning. Start W to turn the rocky spur on which the hut is situated and then ski S down steep slopes (avalanche danger) to cross the L lateral moraine on to the tongue of the A Neuve glacier. Go down the L bank of the Reuse de l'A Neuve stream, away from (S of) the summer path on the R bank of the Reuse de l'Amône stream, to l'A Neuve hamlet and across the River Drance de Ferret to La Fouly in the Ferret valley (1½ h., 8½-9 h. from the Argentière hut).

29   *La Fouly-Bourg St. Pierre*

(a)   Via the Col des Planards. Make sure of an early start. Walk S up the road to Ferret (1705m.), the highest village in the valley (hotels closed in winter). Go SE on the E side of the valley up to Les Ars *Dessus* (1955m.) and climb steep slopes ENE on foot on the R bank of the Vaylat stream, passing between the Clocher de l'Arpalle (2616m.) and the Clocher de la Chaux (2710m.) (spot heights only indicated on LK 50), into the Arpalles basin. Considerable avalanche danger from Les Ars *Dessous* (1802m.) up to 2300m. in warm weather if much snow remains. Now ascend ENE to the Col des Planards (2737m.) (Col Sud des Planards on LK 25), finishing up a steeper slope (4½-5 h.). On the E side of the col descend into the Combe des Planards, turning the first steep rocks R before dropping down into the valley basin which is followed NE towards the Toules lake. At c.2000m. slant NNE to the Letta huts (1908m.). Descend NE on a large track to the old roadhead (1730m.) or go down to the barrage and cross the dam wall (1810m.) to the Great St. Bernard road on the E side of the lake less than 3 km. S of Bourg St. Pierre (6½-8 h. from La Fouly).

(b)   Via the Col du Grand St. Bernard. The Great St. Bernard Pass can be reached from the Swiss Val Ferret by crossing the col at pt.2723m., situated immediately WSW of the Pointe de Drône and known locally as the Col de l'Hiver (named Fenêtre d'en Haut on LK 25, unnamed on LK 50), in preference to the Fenêtre de Ferret which is traversed by the summer path route. Longer in distance but slightly safer than (a). Start as by (a), but continue up the valley beyond Les Ars Dessus. From the Plan de la Chaux (2040m.) climb ESE (avalanche danger) steeply up to the Chaux basin and head SSE on the E side of the Fenêtre lakes over the col (2723m.) to reach the Italian slope of the Great St. Bernard road 1 km. W of the pass. Accommodation available at the hospice (2469m.) (6-6½ h. from La Fouly). On the Swiss side of the pass ski NE down the Combe des Morts to join the piste from the Menouve gondola cableway terminus and N, keeping near the valley bed, to Bourg St. Bernard (1914m.) (½-1 h.), 6 km. S of Bourg St. Pierre.

Italian start to the HLR: Courmayeur-Bourg St. Pierre

An unconventional, long and rarely used route at a comparatively low level links Courmayeur/La Palud directly with the Great St. Bernard Pass. Leave the Italian Val Ferret road (not kept open in winter) just beyond La Vachey (1642m.) and ascend the valley on the R(SE) to the Colle Malatra (2928m.). At the head of the Merdeux cwm, on the other side of the col, pass below the SE spurs of Mont Tapie and the Bella Comba to cross pt.2816m. (named Colle di Saulié on LK 25), the gap at the SE foot of the Piccolo Gollià and immediately NW of the Guglia di Saulié. Traverse the Tula cwm and the Colle di San Rhemy (2560m.) generally E to reach the Great St. Bernard road S of the pass near pt.2079m. (7½-9 h. from road to road). See Route 29(b) for Bourg St. Pierre or, far quicker, continue down ESE and soon reach the S entrance to the Great St. Bernard road tunnel (1875m.). Travel through it (bus service) to Bourg St. Bernard at the Swiss entrance.

Panossière hut-Col du Meitin-Plateau du Couloir-Col de Sonadon-Chanrion hut

Parties who wish first to climb the Grand Combin from the Panossière hut occasionally take this harder route to the Plateau du Couloir. Otherwise it has only disadvantages, for the traverse from the Col du Meitin to the Plateau du Couloir is more delicate and holds a greater avalanche risk than the direct ascent from the Valsorey hut, particularly if negotiated at a later hour in the morning due to the longer approach. To avoid this an early start is essential. Diagram, p. 66.

Access to the Panossière hut is normally from Lourtier by Route 4 or from Fionnay by Route 5.

30   From the Panossière hut follow Route 40 for the Grand Combin to the Maisons Blanches plateau near and W of pt.3406m. Now head S towards the Col du Meitin (3609m.), a prominent snow shoulder on the W ridge of the Combin de Valsorey. In poor visibility take particular care to locate it correctly and not to confuse it with the lower Col des Maisons Blanches to the SW on the other side of the Combin du Meitin. Climb the final slope, which is frequently icy, on foot (4 h.).

Now first descend slightly S and then cross steep exposed slopes SE on foot to the Plateau du Couloir, exiting if possible where the cornice or snow crest meets the rocks of the Combin de Valsorey so as to complete the shortest connection between the two shoulders. In soft snow this section is extremely unpleasant (1-2 h.). Continue by Route 17 (8-10 h. from the Panossière hut to the Chanrion hut).

Panossière hut-Tournelon Blanc-Chanrion hut

Although this traverse was first made at an earlier date than that of the Plateau du Couloir, it has rarely been repeated due to the difficult and dangerous descent on the E side of the Tournelon Blanc. Inadvisable and mentioned primarily for its historical interest. For the Tournelon Blanc from the Panossière hut see p. 115. The route to the Chanrion hut breaks off E at pt.3595m. and leads on foot down a steep narrow unnamed glacier, cut by crevasses, with considerable exposure to avalanches. Below c.3350m. ski generally SE, crossing the

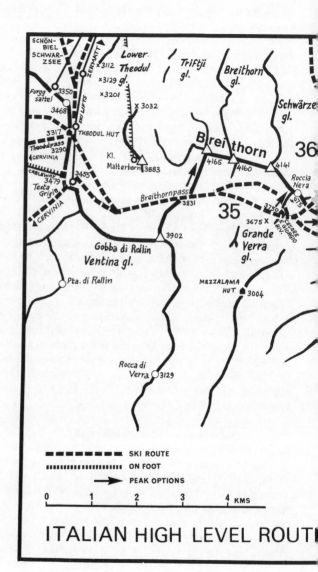

ITALIAN HIGH LEVEL ROUTE

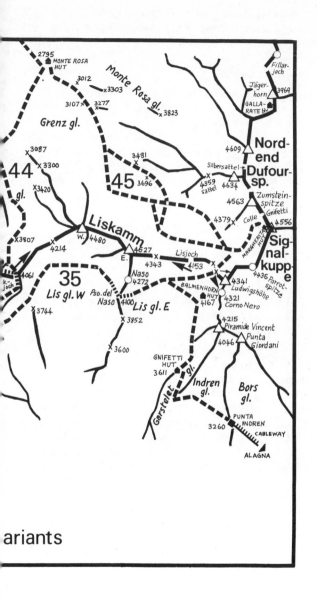

ariants

tongue of the Tsessette glacier, to the Chermotane valley basin at the Lancet bridge (2041m.) and Route 6 (6½-9½ h. from hut to hut).

LITTLE HIGH LEVEL ROUTE

Verbier-Mont Fort hut-Dix hut-Vignettes hut-Zermatt

This line, which links up with the classic HLR at the Vignettes hut, avoids the key passage from the Valsorey hut to the Chanrion hut (Route 17) and in fact forms the normal route for guided groups. It gives equally fine skiing without the same technical difficulties, but nevertheless crosses serious terrain where orientation problems abound in bad weather. An army team lent the alternative name of the Glacier Patrol Route to this tour after reaching Zermatt from Verbier in 36 h. Normally completed in four stages, it is at least as popular and frequented as the classic HLR with superb scenery throughout that is perhaps even more varied.

I. Verbier-Mont Fort hut

See Route 3. Depending on arrival time in Champex at the end of Stage 2 of the classic HLR it may be possible to reach the Mont Fort hut the same day.

II. Mont Fort hut-Dix hut

This strenuous stage can be evenly divided by stopping overnight at the Prafleuri hut, which has become the normal procedure for guided groups. On its central part, between the W foot of the Col de Momin and the Barma huts above the Dix lake, a choice from three options determines whether the Rosablanche is traversed, climbed for its own sake or avoided. Note that the slopes W of the Dix lake below the Rochers du Bouc as well as those at the S end of the lake are sometimes avalanche prone; in that case, sleeping at the Prafleuri hut enables these zones to be passed early in the day with the least danger. If surprised by bad weather in the vicinity of the Dix lake, do not attempt the dangerous descent to Le Chargeur in the Hérémence valley; either continue to the Dix hut or retreat to the Prafleuri hut by the pass at pt.2804m., reversing alternative (ii).

31   From the hut skirt the foot of the Monts de Sion and head SE past pt.2608m. on the moraines to the small Chaux glacier. Ascend its gentle slopes ESE to the Col de la Chaux (2940m.) (1½ h.). Ski down E on the other side into a basin with a small lake (2764m.) at the SW foot of the Petit Mont Fort. Ascend SE, passing below the rock spur that falls W from pt.3059m., to arrive at the W foot of the Col de Momin (1-1½ h.).

There are now three alternative ways to the Barma huts. The first is recommended as the finest, the second enables the stage to be spread over two days but is otherwise more circuitous despite taking no longer, the third gives the shortest connection.

(i) Rosablanche traverse. Head E up to the Col de Momin (3005m.), a depression level with the Grand Désert glacier on its E side. Slant ESE over the gentle upper slopes of this glacier, passing N of the Col de Cleuson, and curve gradually R on steepening terrain to join the broad NE ridge of the Rosablanche (3336m.) which is climbed easily on foot to the summit (1½-2 h., 4-5 h. from hut). Descend the rocks of the S ridge without difficulty on foot. Shortly before the snowy saddle (pt.3196m. on LK 25) between the top and pt.3240m. a short gully leads down L on to the L(N) branch of the small Mourti glacier. A splendid ski run ensues NE straight down the glacier to pt.2766m. below its tongue. Then bear R(ESE), soon reach open slopes and finally the Barma huts (2458m.) after crossing the Ecoulaies glacier stream (1-1½ h.).

(ii) Via the Prafleuri hut. Follow (i) to c.3160m. on the Grand Désert glacier half-way between the Petit Mont Calme and the Rosablanche. (For the addition of the latter peak allow allow ¾-1 h. return). Ski N and NNE down the Prafleuri glacier, keeping nearer its L bank so as to pass L of the rocky humps immediately below its tongue before slanting E over the moraines to the Prafleuri hut by pt.2662m. (1½-2 h., 4-5 h. from the Mont Fort hut). Head gently up the basin S of the hut and ascend a broad gully, sometimes on foot, to the Col des Roux (2804m., as named on LK 50 and also known as the Col de Blava). Now ski down SE to the terrace above the broken rock barrier overlooking the Dix lake. From c.2650m. a shelf conveniently leads SW down to the Ecoulaies glacier valley. Ski SE again, crossing the line of several streams, to the Barma huts (1-1¼ h.).

(iii) Via the Col de Severeu. Ascend SSE to cross the ridge running W from pt.3140m. to the Rochers de Momin at c.2980m. and contour SE before rising slightly towards the Col de la Rionde (3038m., spot height only on LK 50) which is reached over a small plateau. On the other side go down a broad gully, often carrying skis, skirt the W foot of the Rosablanche above two tiny lakes (2868m.) and head SE up the Severeu glacier to the Col de Severeu (3111m.) (1½-2 h.). Ski down E, steeply at first, to the L lateral moraine of the Ecoulaies glacier. Follow it ENE and continue over open slopes in the same direction to the Barma huts (½-1 h.).

From the Barma huts, or slightly above, traverse SSE above the W bank of the Dix lake to pt.2392m. by the Pas du Chat at its S end (1 h.). Jeep road to this point.

Now *either* bear ENE along the head of the lake until a gorge opens to the R from its other tip and leads SE to the slopes below the Cheilon glacier. By spring the snow sometimes builds up to form steep bits in this gorge. Head S to pass R(W) of the rocks marked by pt.2582m. (omitted from new LK 50) and ascend the L bank of the glacier, finally curving R up to the Dix hut (2928m.) on a rocky hump immediately S of the Tête Noire.

Or, given firm snow, go at least half-way along the head of the lake and bear SE up a steep cwm to a promontory marked by pt.2581m. The summer path line which curves in a rising traverse from pt.2392m. up to this point is dangerous in winter/ spring conditions and should only be used if these slopes are largely clear of snow. Follow the L bank moraine of the Cheilon glacier to the foot of the Tête Noire and then move L on to the glacier to join the above approach (2-3 h., 8-10 h. from the Mont Fort hut, 4-5 h. from the Prafleuri hut).

III. Dix hut-Vignettes hut
The ski traverse of the Pigne d'Arolla makes for an outstanding expedition in itself and climaxes the Little HLR. Crevasses have caused several fatal accidents to skiers in recent years hereabouts.

32   From the hut ski down briefly to the Cheilon glacier and cross its central basin SE towards the glacier branch between the Pointes de Tsena Réfien and the rock barrier marked pt. 3029m. This is the badly crevassed R(N) branch of the Tsena Réfien glacier. Climb its steep R(N) bank, keeping near the long rock ridge on the L, until the slopes ease by pt.3423m. and a vaguely defined glacier spur leads SW towards the Col de la Serpentine. Leave this spur at c.3500m. to make a gently rising traverse SE across the next basin where this glacier merges with the Tsidjiore Nouve glacier. SW of pt.3592m. climb a steep slope, the Mur de la Serpentine, on foot. It is sometimes icy and best taken from R to L. Then cross SE to the plateau depression of the Col de Breney (3639m.). Ascend easy slopes ENE to the saddle (c.3740m.) between the Pigne d'Arolla (3796m.) and pt.3772m., then go N to the top (4-5 h.).

Continue to the Vignettes hut as by Route 19 ($\frac{3}{4}$-1$\frac{1}{2}$ h., about 5-6$\frac{1}{2}$ h. from the Dix hut).

IV. Vignettes hut-Zermatt
See Route 20 for Stage 6 of the classic HLR.

Chanrion-Dix huts connection
This route crosses three passes and is mainly taken by parties making for Arolla, though no quicker than going via the Vignettes hut. It also coincides with the approach to Mont Blanc de Cheilon (Route 41). Overall unrewarding from the skiing point of view.

33 From the Chanrion hut head N below the W ridge of the Pointe d'Otemma and NE to pt.2622m. on the L bank moraine of the Breney glacier which is crossed NNE in an upward slant. From the other side ascend fairly steep slopes due N to the Col de Lire Rose (3115m.), a saddle at the R(E) end of a long shoulder (2-3 h.). Go generally N over the small Lire Rose glacier in a slight R-hand curve, finishing up a steeper slope to the Col du Mont Rouge (3335m., 3325m. on new LK 50) (1 h.).

Traverse the broad head of the Giétro glacier NNE, below but on account of avalanche danger not too near to the NW face of La Ruinette, imperceptibly downwards to the Col de Cheilon (3243m.). A short but fine ski run leads NE down the

Cheilon glacier and over its L bank to the Dix hut (1 h., 4-5 h. altogether).

Vignettes-Bertol huts connection

If surprised by bad weather between the Col de l'Evêque and the Col du Mont Brulé on Stage 6 of the classic HLR from the Vignettes hut to Zermatt (Route 20), then a retreat to Arolla becomes the rational solution. However, rather than abandon the traverse entirely, in reasonable conditions parties occasionally cross NW from c.2600m. on the Upper Arolla glacier to soon join the Bertol hut approach (Route 9) just below the Plans de Bertol hut (2665m.) (6-6½ h. from hut to hut). Subject to adequate visibility slightly quicker and far more interesting than skiing directly down to Arolla from the Vignettes hut and then going up to the Bertol hut. N.B. A circuitous HLR, taking in the Tête Blanche, can be effected for its own sake between the two huts: as by Route 20 to the N side of the Col de Valpelline, then reverse Route 34 (7-8 h.).

Arolla-Bertol hut-Tête Blanche-Zermatt

From Arolla the most direct way to Zermatt lies via the Bertol hut and the Tête Blanche. This tour is strongly recommended for its own sake and is mainly undertaken by parties who have reached Arolla from the Dix hut or descended from the Vignettes hut on account of bad weather. Route 20 from the Vignettes hut to Zermatt is joined on the upper slopes of the Stockji glacier. Note that the summer connection across the Col d'Hérens is not normally used on ski.

For the approach to the Bertol hut see Route 9.

34   From the Bertol hut return to the Col de Bertol (3269m.) and slant ESE across the Mont Miné glacier until immediately below pt.3229m. Now head SE over the gentle upper slopes of the glacier towards the Col des Bouquetins. A little before reaching this col, bear E up a shallow cwm parallel to the W ridge of the Tête Blanche (3724m.) and at its head curve R(S) to the summit plateau (2½-3 h.).

In descent ski NE, at first keeping a reasonable distance from the steep drop on the R, to the Col de la Tête Blanche (3596m., unnamed on LK 50). In poor visibility the col, merely a shoulder on the NE ridge providing the easiest passage on to the Stockji glacier, becomes difficult to distinguish as such. N.B. It is slightly quicker to bypass the top of the Tête Blanche by crossing the broad NNW glacier spur of the mtn. ENE directly to this point.

Now double back S and ski fairly steeply on to the upper slopes of the Stockji glacier to join Route 20 from the Vignettes hut a little below and NE of the Col de Valpelline (3-4 h. from the Tête Blanche to Zermatt, 5½-7 h. altogether).

Zermatt-Cervinia
From both resorts mechanical transport rises to and above the Theodulpass. See under Theodul hut on p. 54. Long ski runs over open slopes lead down to Cervinia.

Zermatt-Alagna or Gressoney (Monte Rosa hut-Gnifetti hut)
A complex glacier passage links the Monte Rosa and Gnifetti huts, respectively above these villages. Leave the Grenz glacier approach to the Signalkuppe (Route 45) at c.4180m. and cross the shoulder on the R, situated on the frontier between pt.4260m. and the Ludwigshöhe, before skiing down the L bank of the Lis glacier to the Gnifetti hut (see p. 55) (5½-7 h. from hut to hut).

ITALIAN HIGH LEVEL ROUTE
Theodulpass - Breithornpass - Castor - Felikjoch - Passo del Naso - Monte Rosa hut via Lisjoch/Ludwigshöhe ridge or Gnifetti hut
Between the Breithorn and the Monte Rosa group a magnificent high level line, constantly above 3600m., can be followed on the S side of the frontier ridge. The ridge itself is joined on or near the summit of Castor, at 4226m. the highest point common to both versions of the route, and descended to Felikjoch.

This tour is more serious than and at least as difficult as anything on the classic HLR. More often done in part than as a whole. It should only be undertaken in settled weather. The ascent of Castor by its W flank is comparable with the climb from the Valsorey hut to the Plateau du Couloir. The danger from crevasses must not be underestimated. Even the shortened versions of this tour (Route 35 combined with Route 44, and

Route 36) presume skilful route finding and considerable ski touring experience. Recommended in May or early June for less severe weather conditions. Map, p. 88.

The whole tour is usually divided by breaking off as indicated in the description below to one of the huts near the route, although a very fit and fast party can complete it in a day subject to good conditions and an early start that presupposes sleeping at the Theodul hut. Times quoted do not allow for deep soft snow that is often encountered on a warm afternoon in late spring. Attractive opportunities to climb nearby peaks by detours from the route have to be counterbalanced against the extra time required: possibilities include the Breithorn, Pollux, Liskamm and some of the Monte Rosa summits; it is well worth allowing at least one extra day to take in a few of these peaks. The last part of the route as detailed here covers Swiss ground so that it links up again with the classic HLR and its continuation to Saas Fee, though it is equally possible and in fact easier to finish in Italy as described briefly in N.B.7. An international race (the Mezzalama Trophy) from the Testa Grigia to the Gnifetti hut and below has recently been revived by the Italians and is held biennially in early summer; the record time just exceeds $3\frac{1}{2}$ h!

In the event of bad weather, as far as the W face of Castor the safest retreat lies in retracing one's route despite the problem of orientation on the Breithorn plateau. Alternatively seek shelter in the Cesare e Giorgio bivouac hut (see N.B.2), but do not attempt the descent to the locked Mezzalama hut.

Reach the Theodul hut by uphill transport systems from both Zermatt and Cervinia (see p. 54) or, to incorporate this expedition into the framework of an extended classic HLR without descending to Zermatt, by Route 22 from the Schönbiel hut.

35   From the Theodulpass (3290m.), immediately S of the hut, either ascend the piste to the top of the Testa Grigia ski lift (3455m.) and cross the Plateau Rosa ESE to the glacier basin below the Gobba di Rollin, or head SE directly up the glacier cwm thus far (c.3600m.). The ski lifts hereabouts operate in summer only. Climb a steeper slope ENE from R to L, with crevasses higher up, to the Breithorn plateau which is crossed

E to the Breithornpass (3831m.), the wide saddle marking the lowest point between the Breithorn and the Gobba di Rollin (2-2½ h.). (N.B.1. Access to this pass now takes barely 30 min. from the terminus of the all year Klein Matterhorn cableway. For the Breithorn see Route 43.) Ahead, the route to Castor is now visible.

Ski E down crevassed slopes on to the Grande Verra glacier, losing c.150m. Contour ESE, bewaring of crevasses parallel to the line of march. Pass above pt.3675m. and immediately below the rocks supporting the glacier spur that rises to the frontier ridge slightly W of the Roccia Nera. (N.B.2. The Cesare e Giorgio bivouac hut (c.3750m.) is situated near the top of these rocks, 500m. W of the Schwarztor and   marked on the map. It can be reached by a steep snow slope and a few rocks from the SE or from above by traversing the glacier on a higher terrace between 3750m. and 3850m. For the Roccia Nera see Route 43 N.B.) Bear E gently upwards to the glacier basin on the S side of the Schwarztor (3734m.) (1-1½ h.). (N.B.3. For the Schwärze glacier descent to the Monte Rosa hut see Route 36. For Pollux see p. 123.)

Follow a glacier terrace in a curve immediately below the S foot of Pollux to reach the glacier basin just below and SW of the Zwillingsjoch (3848m.) (½ h.). (N.B.4. The route between this pass and the Monte Rosa hut by the very badly crevassed W branch of the Zwillings glacier is no longer practical. In descent, the invariably icy final slope with a double bergschrund requires abseils.)

Conditions on the W snow/ice face of Castor (4226m.) vary considerably and the best line must be chosen accordingly. Climb the steep slope, initially on ski and later on foot, diagonally R until the angle eases somewhat, directly below the summit. Now either slant back L to reach the narrow summit crest between the fore peak and the top, or continue the ascent from L to R to join the steeper SW ridge a little above 4100m. (1½-2 h.) (5-6½ h. from the Theodul hut). In deep snow avalanche danger sometimes makes it advisable to climb the mtn. by the NW frontier ridge which has a few delicate sections.

Descend on foot without difficulty by the normal route along the SE ridge which finally curves half L down to the Felikjoch

(4071m.) (1 h.). The ridge is often corniced on the R(S side) near the pass. (N.B.5. To descend to the Monte Rosa hut reverse Route 44. For the W peak of the Liskamm see p. 124.)

From the slight dome immediately SE of the Felikjoch go S down a steep slope, on foot or on ski according to the snow conditions, on to the R(W) upper branch of the Felik glacier. Ski SW down gentle slopes between the Punta Perazzi to the R and ice cliffs to the L. Where the ice cliffs peter out at c.3700m. contour E on to the L(E) branch of the glacier ($\frac{1}{2}$ h). (N.B.6. By continuing down SSW the unwardened Quintino Sella hut (3585m.), situated at the top of the long rock ridge dividing the Ayas and Gressoney valleys, is reached in a few min.)

Then slant NE below the ice cliffs to pass above pt.3744m. and below the foot of a rock spur on to the W branch of the Lis glacier. Ascend its R(W) bank and cross the large central terrace E, below the S flank of the Liskamm and well above complex crevasse zones, to the W foot of the Naso (4272m.), an obvious snow dome on the S ridge of the Liskamm. Climb the steep snow/ice flank on foot from L to R and traverse briefly E to arrive c.350m. SSW of the Naso at the so-called Passo del Naso (c.4100m., not marked on map) ($2\frac{1}{2}$-3 h.). This is not a pass but rather the sole practical crossing point on the ridge.

Descend a short steep slope E and cross a bergschrund on to the E branch of the Lis glacier before bearing ENE towards the frontier ridge between the Lisjoch and the Ludwigshöhe. (N.B.7. For the Gnifetti hut cross the glacier by a L-hand curve to the foot of the Balmenhorn rock island (4167m.), the site of a bivouac hut and a prominent statue of Christ, and ski S down the E bank cwm below the Piramide Vincent (1-1$\frac{1}{2}$ h. from the Passo del Naso, at least 10-13 h. from the Theodul hut).) Continue in the same direction over gentle slopes to a shoulder (4246m. on LK 25) on the frontier immediately R of pt.4260m. and L(NW) of the Ludwigshöhe (1$\frac{1}{2}$-2 h.). Note that the Lisjoch is not crossed due to the impassable ice cliff on the Swiss side. (N.B.8. The Corno Nero, Ludwigshöhe and Parrotspitze offer short ascents hereabouts: see notes on p. 125. For the Signalkuppe see Route 45.)

Ski NE across the Grenz glacier and soon join the Signalkuppe (Margherita hut) approach at c.4180m. Reverse Route 45 down the glacier and finally its R bank moraines to the Monte Rosa hut (1-1½ h., at least 11½-15 h. from the Theodul hut and allow longer). 2 h. less from top of K1. Matterhorn cableway.

Theodulpass-Breithornpass-Castor-Felikjoch-Monte Rosa hut
In practice most parties break off the Italian HLR at the Felikjoch and during a period of fine weather the ski run to the Monte Rosa hut is almost always tracked, thus eliminating route finding problems on the complex Zwillings glacier. Follow Route 35 to the Felikjoch (6-7½ h.) and then reverse Route 44 (1-2 h., 7-9½ h. altogether).

Theodulpass-Breithornpass-Schwarztor-Monte Rosa hut
The shortest high level traverse by passes on the frontier between the Theodul and Monte Rosa huts. Good visibility is an essential prerequisite for the descent of the badly crevassed Schwärze glacier which presents serious problems after a winter devoid of substantial snowfalls.

36   Follow Route 35 to the Schwarztor (3-4 h.).

Traverse very briefly NE towards the N ridge of Pollux and then ski N down the gently inclined upper basin of the Schwärze glacier. These fairly harmless slopes belie the nature of the descent. However, below c.3500m. the slope steepens abruptly. Take care not to continue too far down the centre of the glacier which soon becomes an impassable icefall. This is not obvious from above. Instead, cross half R to the narrow slope immediately L(W) of pt.3398m., but keep well away from the R edge which is bordered by ice cliffs. Between 3300m. and 3150m. the best line through the icefall varies from year to year according to the state of the glacier, but generally trend slightly R to reach the open slopes below; in places it may be necessary to carry skis. Now ski down the R bank of the glacier which gives a fine run despite the crevasses. Pass pt.2632m. at the NW foot of the Schwärze to reach the L bank of the Gorner glacier by its junction with the Grenz glacier. Ascend gently E, working towards the centre of the glacier, then SE to the height of the Monte Rosa hut before crossing horizontally L(NE) between crevasses on the R bank and finally over the moraine crest to it (2-3 h., 5-7 h. altogether).

Zermatt-Saas Fee

Contrary to summer practice ski tourers cross almost exclusively by the Adlerpass: see Routes 23-26. In either direction uphill transport shortens this approach. Until late spring access to the Täsch hut, the starting-point for the Alphubeljoch or the Allalinpass, requires particular care on the final steep slope from the valley bed and one should not attempt the rising traverse line of the jeep road from the Täschalp inn. From the hut the more direct route across the Alphubeljoch (3782m.) is normally preferred to the circuitous way via the Allalinpass (3564m.), a trend that would increase in reverse if the proposed extension of the Saas Fee cableway system to the Feekopf is built: see Route 50. The Allalinpass can also be reached straight from the Täschalp by the Mellich stream and glacier, a more interesting and practical possibility in reverse if going from the Britannia hut to Täsch.

Zermatt or Monte Rosa hut-Schwarzberg-Weisstor-Saas Almagell

The shortest route to the Saas valley across the Schwarzberg-Weisstor is little used nowadays due to the popularity of the Adlerpass. None the less a fine ski tour amidst remote surroundings despite uphill transport at the start.

The term Schwarzberg-Weisstor is designated to the approx. 700m. long ridge between the S foot of the Strahlhorn and the junction with the frontier ridge at pt.3609m. (named Schwarzberghorn on LK 25, trig. marker). Pt. 3609m. must not be confused with either the snow dome marked pt.3641m. or the Neue Weisstorspitze (3636m., unnamed on map), a far more prominent top rising immediately above the Neues Weisstor on the continuation SSW of the ridge that is known as the Weissgrat. From the W side it is not apparent where the frontier ridge breaks off E. Due to a rock face on its E flank the actual pass (3537m.) is not crossed but instead pt.3609m., a rock knoll forming the highest point at its S limit that marks the start of the mtn. chain dividing the Saas and Zermatt valleys. Crevassed glaciers on both sides.

The construction of the Mattmark lake in connection with hydro-electric schemes during the 1960s has created spring problems for ski tourers. The banks of the lake are sometimes exposed to considerable avalanche danger and the tunnels reducing this risk may be blocked but are normally passable in spring; check locally.

37   Reach the Stockhornpass (3394m., variable on LK 50) from Zermatt by Route 24 (1 h. from the cableway terminus) or from the Monte Rosa hut by Route 23 (3-3½ h.).

A direct contouring movement ENE below the NW slopes of the Cima di Jazzi to the upper plateau of the Findeln glacier is often seriously complicated by large crevasse zones. A far better route is found by first ascending a broad glacier spur SE towards pt.3636m. (Torre di Castelfranco on LK 25). The spur is a continuation of the Stockhorn ridge between the Findeln and Gorner glaciers. Coming from the Monte Rosa hut this spur can be joined straight from the Gorner glacier by continuing E below the Stockhornpass. Leave it at c.3500m. and traverse NE up to the broad NW glacier spur of the Cima di Jazzi at c.3600m. Ski NE in a downward slant below the Neues Weisstor, an obvious wide saddle on the R, and rise slightly across the upper basin of the Findeln glacier to the W foot of pt.3609m. on the Schwarzberg-Weisstor. Climb a short snow slope and a few rocks to this point (1½-2 h., 2½-3 h. from Zermatt excl. travelling time, 4½-5½ h. from the Monte Rosa hut).

N.B.   Another feasible but longer approach from Zermatt starts as by Route 25 and continues up the R bank of the Findeln glacier (4-4½ h. from Blauherd).

Scramble E along the frontier ridge and after c.300m. break off L(N) on to the Schwarzberg glacier. Descend the initial steep slope on foot and cross a bergschrund. Ski down the crevassed upper basin briefly and head NE down the terraced glacier to reach the R bank at c.2900m. If the crevasses are insufficiently covered, then bear ENE earlier towards pt.3074m. on the ridge above the R bank. Pass R of the rock barrier at c.2700m. and continue skiing NNE down the steep moraine slopes to the jeep track above the L(W) shore of the Mattmark lake at c.2240m. (1½ h.).

N.B. Older editions of the LK 50 incl. the ski routes version do not show the Schwarzberg glacier in its current state: it has receded to c.2660m. The Mattmark lake is likewise not indicated. Consult the LK 25 for up-to-date detail.

Follow the jeep road, passing through two tunnels well below the Schwarzbergalp, to the dam at the N end of the lake. If these tunnels are blocked by snow, then avalanche danger probably threatens the awkward traverse above the W shore: see introductory preamble. The contractors' road immediately crosses to the R side of the Saaser Vispa river and leads down to Saas Almagell (1672m.). The time taken from the lake varies according to the presence of snow and the road is not officially open until June (1-2 h., 2½-3½ h. from the Schwarzberg-Weisstor, 5-6½ h. from Zermatt via Stockhorn or 6½-8 h. via Blauherd, 7-9 h. from the Monte Rosa hut).

Zermatt-Macugnaga (Staffa)
From the Schwarzberg-Weisstor (Route 37) a traverse E on the Swiss side of the frontier ridge along the head of the Schwarzberg and Seewjinen glaciers, gradually losing height, leads to the Monte Moro (2984m.) and down its E ridge on foot to the Monte Moropass (2868m.) (2½-3 h.). The cableway terminus is situated c.50m. below the pass to the W. Piste runs to Macugnaga (1307m.) or the intermediate station in spring (6-7 h. from Zermatt). A finer expedition in reverse and quicker by skiing down the Findeln glacier. No alternative ski route connects the two resorts directly.

Britannia hut-Längfluh inn connection
This link is relevant in preparation for shorter ascents of the Allalinhorn and Alphubel. The route described below also corresponds with the Britannia hut approach to these two peaks.

38 From the Britannia hut cross the upper slopes of the Kessjen glacier NW to the Egginerjoch (2991m.) and on the other side ski down a cwm in the same direction (piste). At c.2830m. bear W across the Fee glacier and pass below the Felskinn cableway terminus on the rock island marked by pt. 2990m. to a flat glacier basin. Alternatively reach this point from the Egginerjoch by traversing 50m. above the Felskinn and descending a steep slope NW, at first on foot (safety nets). Slant WNW upwards, immediately N of the rock buttress marked pt.3081m., to a plateau on the broad glacier cwm that rises N to the Feejoch. Cross briefly W above the icefall and from c.3050m. ski SSW down gentle slopes to the Längfluh inn (2870m.) ($1\frac{1}{2}$-2 h.).

PART V

MOUNTAINS

Numbered route descriptions are limited to the major ski peaks. Other ski tops situated near the HLR and its alternatives are dealt with in comprehensive note form and for these summits no practical ski routes have been omitted. A few ski runs from mtns. served by cableways have been incorporated here for their special interest to the ski tourer. Ski mountaineering possibilities, incl. hut approaches as appropriate, in other areas of the Mont Blanc Range and the Pennine Alps are summarized to complete the survey. Some of the routes merely mentioned here are indicated on the LK 50 ski maps and detailed tersely on the reverse sides. Fuller details about many of these latter peaks are found in the Alpine Club guidebooks to the Mont Blanc Range and the Pennine Alps.

A. MONT BLANC RANGE

TRÉLATÊTE GROUP

Ski approaches to these peaks at the W limits of the range start from Les Contamines (small CAF chalet here) in the French Montjoie valley with a 3½ h. ascent to the Trélatête hotel (1970m.) which is normally open in spring with a simple restaurant service. Some splendid long ski runs are available in the vicinity which remains totally unspoilt by mechanized uphill transport. The unwardened Conscrits hut (2730m.), a primitive box-like shelter equipped with ten mattresses but no blankets and situated on the Trélagrande (R) bank of the Trélatête glacier, serves as a higher base and is reached from the hotel over the glacier in 2½-3 h.

The Col Infranchissable gives the easiest ski run, while the *Dôme de Miage* (3673m.) and the *Aig. de la Bérangère* (3425m.) offer the most rewarding ascents with fine views. From the latter peak expert skiers sometimes descend by the steep Armancette glacier on the N side directly to Les Contamines, a difficult and complex run starting from the Col de la Bérangère. In good snow conditions the *Tête Carrée*, *Aig. de Trélatête* N peak and *Mont Tondu* can be climbed most of the way on ski.

The *Aig. des Glaciers* (3816m.), via the Col des Glaciers and the SW ridge, is a serious undertaking with some mixed climbing on the final rocks above the Dôme de Neige. Yet in the Trélatête group only this summit can be approached on ski from the Italian Val Veni (Courmayeur) via the Col de la Seigne and the Glaciers glacier; it is also possible to join this route from the Chapieux valley to the SW.

MONT BLANC   4807m.

The highest mtn. in the Alps is covered by a complex system of large glaciers on the Chamonix side. A broad snow crest marks its summit which sends out six major ridges. One of these, the Bosses Ridge, provides the most reliable way to the top. In winter/spring the approach to this ridge from Chamonix via the Grands Mulets hut offers ski mountaineers a magnificent expedition which makes an ideal climax to a holiday and presents no technical difficulties in ideal conditions. However, an ascent of Mont Blanc on ski always remains a serious undertaking that should only be attempted by experienced ski mountaineers. The dangers of a long expedition at high altitude are far greater in winter/spring than in summer. Particular respect should be paid to the intense cold which exaggerates the effect of any minor mishap. Strong winds on the Bosses Ridge and below have obliged many parties to retreat. Oncoming bad weather must never be ignored. While the extensive summit panorama takes in the entire Western Alps, individual mtns. appear less significant from a higher viewpoint.

Suitable conditions for an ascent of Mont Blanc rarely prevail in winter or even early spring. The state of the glaciers generally improves as the snow consolidates during the skiing season. In an average year the best time lies between late April and mid-June. In late spring and early summer helicopter flights are at times organized to land skiers on the Col du Dôme.

First ascent: J. Balmat and M. G. Paccard, 8 August 1786.

First winter ascent, by the Grands Mulets and Bosses Ridge: Miss A. Straton with M. Balmat, J. E. Charlet and S. Couttet, 31 January 1876. First ski ascent: H. Mylius with K. Maurer, A Tännler and H. Zurfluh, 25 February 1904.

Grands Mulets Route, via the Bosses Ridge. The traditional way up and by far the best ski route. Skis are left at the Vallot hut. The danger from crevasses should not be underestimated. Fitness and prior acclimatization are essential for the enjoyment of this undertaking which may otherwise be found exhausting. Reliable estimates suggest that of those who set out from the hut well over 50 per cent turn back below the top, above all at the Vallot hut. During a spell of fine weather in late spring the route will almost inevitably be well tracked. In poor visibility, however, special care must be exercised not to lose the route in the vicinity of the Col du Dôme and the Grand Plateau. If the snow still extends down to Chamonix (rarely the case in spring, see Route 1), then this is the greatest vertical interval covered by any ski run in the Alps.

It is possible to take the cableway from the Plan de l'Aiguille up to the Aig. du Midi, then ski down the Vallée Blanche (see p. 108), a splendid finale after an ascent of Mont Blanc.

39   From the Grands Mulets hut (3051m.) slant SW from L to R up the crevassed glacier towards some rocks jutting out from the N ridge of the Dôme du Goûter which encloses this branch of the glacier on the R(W). On the L it is bounded hereabouts by the Pic Wilson and the Rocher de l'Heureux Retour. Once near the ice cliffs of the Dôme du Goûter, climb a steep snow slope (the Petites Montées) slightly L up to the Petit Plateau (c.3650m.). Cross this shelf, keeping away from the ice cliffs on the R on account of the danger of falling séracs, and then ascend another steep slope (the Grandes Montées). At the top of this cross large crevasses generally on the R to reach the large snowfield of the Grand Plateau (c.3980m.). This section is also exposed to ice avalanches from the R. Now head WSW up to the broad saddle of the Col du Dôme (c.4250m.), situated SE of the nearby indistinct summit of the Dôme du

Goûter (4304m.). Bear L(SE) up to the Vallot hut on a small prominent rock outcrop (the Rochers Foudroyés) (5-6 h.). Skis are left here or sometimes at the Col du Dôme if the slope below the hut has been swept bare.

Above the hut the slope soon steepens and merges into the Bosses (NW) ridge. Follow this ridge over two snow humps, the Grande Bosse (4513m.) and the Petite Bosse (4547m.), and descend slightly into a dip. Continue up the ridge, passing to the L of the Rochers de la Tournette (4677m.), until a narrow snow crest finally leads to the top ($1\frac{1}{2}$-$2\frac{1}{2}$ h., $6\frac{1}{2}$-$8\frac{1}{2}$ h. from the Grands Mulets hut).

Corridor Route. In very favourable conditions the summit of Mont Blanc can be reached on ski by this route. However, beware especially of slab avalanches in the Corridor. From the Grand Plateau (Route 39) head ESE, passing S of a rognon (3928m.), and climb the Corridor almost to the Col de la Brenva (4303m.). It is far safer to carry skis. Trend R to the Mur de la Côte, a steep 100m. snow/ice slope, which must usually be taken on foot (crampons). Broad snow slopes now lead to the top (6-9 h. altogether).

N.B. From the Col de la Brenva one can climb *Mont Maudit* (4465m.) without difficulty by its S slopes and ridge in $\frac{3}{4}$-1 h.

From the Col du Midi via Mont Blanc du Tacul. Despite access by cableways from both Chamonix and Courmayeur to the Aig. du Midi this route to Mont Blanc is infrequently taken by ski mountaineers and then mainly in early summer. An enforced retreat in bad weather presents serious problems and skis must be carried much of the way. Accommodation is usually available at the Laboratoire (3613m.) above (N of) the Col du Midi (3532m.). The N slopes of *Mont Blanc du Tacul* (4248m.) are ascended mainly on foot to the W shoulder (avalanche danger at times). A 30 min. detour leads easily to its summit. Descend slightly S into a broad basin and climb steep slopes on foot either to the Col du Mont Maudit (4354m.) or to *Mont Maudit* according to the state of the bergschrunds. Continue via the Col de la Brenva to Mont Blanc ($8\frac{1}{2}$-11 h. from the Laboratoire).

From the Italian Miage glacier. The summer approach from Courmayeur via Lake Combal and the Miage glacier to the Gonella hut is exceedingly dangerous in winter conditions. Moreover, the long ridge between the Col des Aigs. Grises and the Dôme du Goûter must be followed on foot. This approach offers the ski mountaineer little reward. An ascent by the Miage and Italian Bionnassay glaciers (enormous crevasse zones around 2900m.) to the Col de Bionnassay, then E to the Dôme du Goûter, requires a bivouac but is possible and gives more skiing than the Dôme glacier route. Rarely undertaken.

AIGUILLE DU MIDI   3842m.

The highest point of the Chamonix Aiguilles and a spectacular viewpoint. Since the construction of cableways from Chamonix and Courmayeur to this summit the ski descent of the Vallée Blanche has become the most famous spring ski run in the Alps. None the less it should not be treated as a normal piste and is not advertised as such by the authorities. Numerous crevasses form a constant danger to the unwary, especially before fresh snow has consolidated. Louis Lachenal, conqueror of Annapurna I in 1950, was killed by a fall into a crevasse on this run. Many ski mountaineers nowadays use this descent as a form of training for the HLR.

From Chamonix the 14 min. journey to the N peak is made in two stages via the Plan de l'Aiguille. The connecting cableway from Italy arrives just below on a terrace overlooking the Vallée Blanche. From the upper station tunnels lead out on to a short snow ridge which is followed down to the glacier.

The run starts with a short steep slope and then crosses the broad head of the Vallée Blanche SE to the Col du Gros Rognon (3415m.) at the W foot of the Gros Rognon. It leads ESE down the pleasant slopes of the Géant glacier, later curving N to the crevassed Bédière plateau. Continuing in the same direction the hardest section of the run, the complex Géant icefall, is reached. Unsure skiers often cause delays here. Below the Requin hut the Tacul glacier is joined and this in turn runs into the Mer de Glace. Given sufficient snow the skiing is now very easy, otherwise icy patches can be unpleasant. While the snow lasts the piste continues down via Le Chapeau to Le Lavancher or Les Tines on the Chamonix-Argentière road. Once the snow has melted below 1800m. go up to the Montenvers and descend on foot. The cable lift from the glacier up to the Montenvers only runs in conjunction with the rack railway from Chamonix which does not operate fully until June.

POINTE HELBRONNER   3462m.

This secondary top is served by the cableways linking La Palud (Courmayeur) with the Aig. du Midi and Chamonix. It acts as the frontier terminus and is situated above (W of) the Col du Géant (3365m.), the best known glacier pass in the Mont Blanc Range. Accommodation and meals are available just below at the CAI's Torino hotel or hut; short cableway connection. Summer skiing facilities abound on the N facing slopes.

To join the 18 km. ski run from the Aig. du Midi to Chamonix, either head straight down the Géant glacier on the R(E) of La Vierge to the Bédière plateau or, longer, first cross the Col des Flambeaux and then take the glacier's W branch.

On the Italian side the only ski route gives a steep run with a roundabout start; not a conventional piste, good conditions essential. Cross the Col des Flambeaux and contour the NW flank of the Grand Flambeau before rising slightly to the Col de Toule E (3410m., E of the Aig. de Toule). After a short descent on foot to the Toule glacier ski steeply towards its L bank and later cross the moraine L to the Mont Fréty slopes. Near the Pavilion cableway station bear steeply SE and finally curve SW past the Chapy huts to La Palud (1370m.).

CENTRAL AREA

Ski mountaineering opportunities in the central part of the Mont Blanc Range are strictly limited. On the approach to the *Tour Ronde* (3792m.), a first-class viewpoint, skis are useful as far as the slope below the Col Freshfield. In favourable snow conditions the *Aig. du Plan* (3673m.), the second highest of the Chamonix Aiguilles, can be climbed on ski from the Requin hut up the steep Envers du Plan glacier to the Col Supérieur du Plan and the summit rocks are quite easy. On the *Aig. du Tacul* (3444m.), also approached from the Requin hut, skis can be used up the Périades glacier to c.3200m. at the foot of the couloir coming down from the Col du Tacul N; from the col the SE ridge is climbed to the top.

A ski ascent of the *Aig. de Rochefort* (4001m.) from the Leschaux hut by the L(W) bank of the chaotic Mont Mallet glacier undoubtedly offers the most outstanding expedition hereabouts, especially in terms of magnificent wild scenery (7-9 h.). It should only be undertaken by the very experienced after a snowy winter has adequately covered the innumerable crevasses. The final huge bergschrund at the head of the glacier is usually difficult and sometimes impassable. N.B. The Périades biv. hut is insufficiently equipped for winter use but does offer shelter in an emergency.

Access to the Couvercle hut in spring is often dangerous, but ski tourers do occasionally visit the Col de Triolet from where the *Pointe Isabella* (3761m.) merely involves a short scramble by its NE ridge. The altogether more serious *Aig. de Triolet* (3870m.) requires technical skills and particular care on the S flank traverse to the upper col immediately below the peak.

ARGENTIÈRE GROUP

Although only the Col du Chardonnet can be traversed on ski from the Argentière hut into Switzerland (Route 12), two other passes further S on the frontier ridge are accessible from the French side and give fine ski runs. The Améthystes glacier, the scene of an annual ski race, leads up to the Col du Tour Noir (3534m.). For the Col d'Argentière (3552m.) cross the bottom of the Améthystes glacier and ascend the Tour Noir glacier E to the col. Above, it sometimes becomes feasible to climb the *Tour Noir* (3835m.) by its S ridge and SE flank (a few pitches II) in late spring, as the snow clears quickly from the rocks during fine weather. N.B. The original summer HLR crossed into Switzerland at the Passage d'Argentière (3620m.), a shoulder 200m. N above the Col d'Argentière and impracticable in winter/spring conditions.

Good snow conditions permit an ascent of the *Aig. d'Argentière* (3900m.) by the Milieu glacier on its SW flank. Skis are left at c.3600m. by the bergschrund below the steep upper slopes (4-5 h. from the Argentière hut).

Mont Dolent (3823m.) rises inaccessibly above the SE head of the Argentière glacier basin. However, for the experienced ski mountaineer a roundabout approach leads SW from La Fouly (1593m.) by the Combe des Fonds to the Petit Col Ferret (2490m.) and traverses below pt.2515m. before slanting NW up to the Fiorio bivouac hut (2720m.). 18 bunks.

N.B. Avalanche danger precludes the steep approach from the Italian Val Ferret until fairly clear of snow. From the biv. hut the E branch of the Pré de Bar glacier is ascended on ski to the bergschrund at c.3600m., then climb a snow ridge and the gully on its R to the summit crest (8-10 h. from La Fouly). The Swiss usually prefer to complete this tour in a day by means of a very early start.

PLATEAU DU TRIENT

Several of the minor summits above the Trient glacier plateau offer short ski tours from the Albert Premier and Trient huts, with short scrambles to finish.

The *Aig. du Tour* (3540m.) is distinguished by a choice of approaches to the easy final rocks on the E side of the S peak. 2-2½ h. suffices to the top from the Trient hut and 3-3½ h. from the Albert Premier hut via the Col du Tour, see Route 27. For the route from Le Tour by the Grands glacier, as described on p. 83, allow 4-5 h. Time and fitness factors argue against a detour to take in this peak during Stage 2 of the classic HLR from the Argentière hut to Champex (Route 12).

To climb either the *Petite Fourche* (3512m.) or the *Tête Blanche* (3421m.) make a 1-1½ h. digression from below the Col du Tour off Route 27 coming up from the Albert Premier hut and reach the latter level summit on ski. On the former a short rock scramble leads to the top.

For *Le Portalet* (3344m.) head S over the glacier from the Trient hut to cross the V-shaped Col N des Plines (not marked on map), immediately NE of the Roc des Plines (3294m.), on to the Ravines Rousses glacier. Contour to the W flank which is climbed, leaving skis about half-way up, to join either ridge near the summit (2-2½ h.).

Immediately N above the Trient hut the *Pointe d'Orny* (3269m.) can be reached by an easy slope in 20 min.

The open expanse of the Plateau du Trient makes it an ideal landing place for flights arranged in spring to give skiers glacier runs without any prior exertion.

B. PENNINE ALPS

MONT VÉLAN   3734m.

A beautiful snow dome with fine glacier skiing on N facing slopes. Set apart from other peaks of similar height, the summit panorama is extensive and includes a most informative view of the route from the Valsorey hut via the Plateau du Couloir to the Col de Sonadon (HLR Stage 4).

For the Vélan hut (2569m.) leave the Valsorey hut approach (Route 16) near pt.2238m. beyond the Chalet d'Amont and head steeply S, or in doubtful snow slant up to the L bank moraine of the Tseudet glacier (3½-4 h.). N.B. An alternative high level approach from Bourg St. Bernard traverses the Croix de Tsousse.

From the hut the ascent leads up the Tseudet glacier to the Col de la Gouille which is crossed on foot to the Valsorey glacier. Snow or ice often conceals the fixed chains here in spring, so belays may be necessary. Turn crevasse zones according to the conditions, trending towards the frontier ridge to reach the top from the SE (4½-6 h.).

To join Route 16 to the Valsorey hut cross from the Vélan hut on to the Tseudet glacier and ski NE to the R bank moraine of the Valsorey glacier (2½-3 h. from hut to hut).

PETIT COMBIN   3672m.
COMBIN DE CORBASSIÈRE   3715m.
COMBIN DE BOVEYRE   3663m.

These three satellites of the Grand Combin have similar approaches from the Panossière hut and the first two are frequently combined. Taken individually allow at least 4 h. each. Varied skiing in fine surroundings.

Start SSW and ascend the L bank of the Corbassière glacier until just S of pt.3155m. before curving R to head NW up a large glacier bay. This way is easier than the line N of pt.3155m. indicated on the LK 50 ski map. Continue NW up to the obvious gap (3563m.) immediately R of pt.3622m. at the foot of the

Combin de Corbassière W ridge which is followed on foot to the summit. From the gap descend very slightly and cross the enclosed upper plateau of the Follats glacier NNW to reach the top of the Petit Combin on ski by its SW slope. N.B. In suitable conditions (plenty of firm snow) expert skiers occasionally descend the steep and crevassed R branch of the Follats glacier.

For the Combin de Boveyre head W from c.3300m. at the entrance to the aforesaid glacier bay to the Col de Panossière (3458m.), climbing the final steep mixed slope on foot, and go up the N ridge to the summit.

N.B. In late spring Swiss weekenders often favour the long approach from the Great St. Bernard road to the Col de Panossière, described briefly in reverse on p. 81 under the Stage 7 note to the HLR East to West.

GRAND COMBIN   4314m.

The Grand Combin stands aloof as the highest and most dominant mtn. between the Matterhorn and Mont Blanc. Four peaks crown this massif: in the E the insignificant snow shoulder of the Combin de Tsessette (4141m.), above the steep slope of the Mur de la Côte the Aig. du Croissant (4243m., not marked on LK 50) with the culminant Combin de Grafeneire immediately behind and finally the westerly Combin de Valsorey (4184m).

The two sides of the main peak contrast markedly: the rugged S face falls 700m. to the Plateau du Couloir, the key passage on the HLR, while the N side is formed of gigantic hanging glaciers divided by a number of terraces. The only practical ski route leads up the so-called Corridor, a glacier band and the sole weakness in this impressive mass of ice. On this section unavoidable dangers, namely the threat of ice avalanches and falling séracs, are encountered. Skiing conditions here vary considerably and are often most favourable after a snowfall, as ice debris may otherwise mar the run. Above, even in spring the Mur de la Côte, a 50m. snow/ice flank, may be icy and forms the crux. The combination of height, length, danger and difficulty makes this a serious yet magnificent expedition that ranks highly in ski mountaineering circles. Comparable in standard, features and nomenclature with the Corridor Route on Mont Blanc (see p. 107).

The popular summer climb by the W ridge of the Combin de Valsorey from the Col du Meitin is a non-starter in winter conditions. Suitable conditions for the mixed SW flank route to the same peak from the Plateau du Couloir rarely prevail.

40   From the Panossière hut the best way up the Corbassière glacier varies according to its state. Plenty of snow usually favours the first option. Concealed crevasses require care.

(i)   Go straight up the R(E) bank of the glacier, passing near and W of pt.3140m., to the Maisons Blanches plateau, reached near and W of pt.3406m. by a steeper slope.

(ii) Cross the glacier SSW to the vicinity of pt.2840m. on the L bank which is followed in the same direction until immediately S of pt.3155m.   Then ascend a bay briefly W towards the Combin de Boveyre before heading S across the Maisons Blanches plateau to arrive near pt.3406m. (3-3½ h.).

N.B.1.   From the Valsorey hut it is possible but harder to reach this point equally quickly by climbing steep slopes NE to the Col du Meitin and then reversing Route 30.   Not recommended, and unpleasant in descent.

Now bear L up the Plateau du Déjeuner, a broad glacier terrace sloping SE above the crescent-shaped rock barrier at the N foot of the massif.   Keep nearer to its outer edge to pass above pt.3555m. at the top of the rock barrier.   Continue more steeply SE up the narrower glacier band of the Corridor, exposed to possible avalanches from overhanging ice cliffs.   Towards 4000m. at its upper end turn a crevassed zone L(E) before doubling back R(SW) to the foot of the Mur de la Côte by the Col du Croissant (4090m., not named on map) (2-2½ h.).   Skis are left here.

N.B.2.   To the E undulating slopes lead easily to the Combin de Tsessette in ½ h.

Climb the Mur de la Côte obliquely from L to R to reach the summit plateau.   In icy conditions cut steps or be prepared to abseil from ice pegs on the descent.   Now *either* follow the main ridge which is corniced on the L, first S, traversing the Aig. du Croissant (4243m., marked on LK 25 only), and climb SSW to the Combin de Grafeneire, *or* (easier) contour SW across the plateau before bearing L(SE) up a straightforward snow slope to the summit (1½-2 h., 6½-8 h. altogether).

N.B.3. To take in the Combin de Valsorey as well, cross the entire plateau SW to join its E ridge very near the top, return along the ridge to the broad saddle at pt.4131m. and reach the Grafeneire by its W ridge or the slope on the L (½ h. extra).

TOURNELON BLANC   3707m.

The interesting roundabout route to this summit from the Panossière hut requires competent skiing and mountaineering techniques. Ascend the R bank of the Corbassière glacier past pt.3140m. before bearing steeply L up the crevassed W slopes of the Mulets de Tsessette to the Col du Tournelon Blanc (3538m., named on LK 25 only); subject to good conditions on the descent this section highlights an exhilerating ski run. Now follow the humpy SW snow ridge to the depression at pt.3595m., then keep slightly R and finish on foot by the short S slope (4-4½ h.). See also the note on p. 87 about the dangerous traverse to the Chanrion hut.

MONT FORT   3328m.

A recommended ski tour from the Mont Fort hut, sometimes undertaken when unsettled weather renders the long traverse to the Dix hut inadvisable. Regrettably, for the tourer, high level cableways to this peak from Tortin and Verbier via Mont Gelé or the Monts de Sion have been discussed for some years. These would open up more first-class piste skiing but spoil the immediate surroundings. This ambitious project has now been postponed for several years at least. Climbed by crossing the Col des Gentianes (2891m.) to the upper slopes of the Tortin glacier which are ascended to the short SW ridge (3 h.). N.B. To complete a delightful round trip ski down the N slopes to Tortin and return by the cableway network via the Col de Chassoure and Les Attelas or Mont Gelé to the hut.

ROSABLANCHE   3336m.

An inconspicuous mtn. but none the less of particular interest to the ski tourer, with four different approaches. Very frequently traversed from the Mont Fort hut to the Dix hut by parties going from Verbier to Zermatt, and vice versa: see Route 31. The longest and finest ski descent, over the N slopes by the appropriately named Grand Désert glacier and the upper Nendaz (Cleuson) valley with a brief re-ascent to Tortin, remains the least used due to the general preference for connecting hut to hut tours. From the Mont Fort hut, 4-5 h. From the Prafleuri hut, 2-2½ h. From the Dix hut, 5-6 h.

LA LUETTE   3548m.

By far the easiest ascent from the Dix hut and an ideal training tour with a pleasant run; suitable for a short day or as an afternoon rucksack-free bonus after coming up from Arolla and sometimes even after completing a traverse from another hut. Head WSW to and W over the Luette glacier to join the SE ridge at a snow saddle NW of pt.3444m. Follow the crest easily to the summit (2 h.).

MONT BLANC DE CHEILON   3869m.

The tremendous N face of the mtn. is the show-piece of the Dix hut. The interesting and varied ski ascent by its circuitous W flank route is strongly recommended to parties with Alpine mountaineering experience. Note that this approach differs from the usual summer route. In very good conditions skis are used beyond the saddle between the SW fore peak and the summit.

41   From the hut go SW across the moraines to the Cheilon glacier and ascend its L bank to the Col de Cheilon (3243m.) (1¼ h.). Traverse the broad head of the Giétro glacier SSE, then bear L up the steep glacier cwm R(S) of pt.3359m. and below the NE face of La Ruinette. Large crevasses sometimes require detours which should not be made too far L where the slope is threatened by séracs. Continue upwards in a R-hand curve to reach a broad glacier ramp that leads NE, parallel to the SW ridge of the mtn., up to the snow dome of the fore peak (3827m.). Generally leave skis here. However, provided that the W slopes are not icy, one can turn the fore peak L and keep below the crest to join the ridge at the foot of the summit riser beyond the saddle between the two peaks. Climb the narrow rock ridge, often corniced and icy, to the top (4½-5 h. from the hut).

Coming from the Chanrion hut by Route 33, break off R(E) on to this approach from due N of La Ruinette (6-7½ h. to the summit).

LA RUINETTE   3875m.

The highest point hereabouts; extensive views. Occasionally ascended on ski from the Chanrion hut by leaving the Breney glacier (Route 19) at c.2900m. to head NW up steep slopes, passing immediately L of pt.3050.3m., and the Ruinette glacier to a flat saddle on the SW shoulder between pt.3710m. and the summit on the R. The SW ridge gives a short, steep climb to the top (5½-6 h.). A serious expedition in a remote situation.

PIGNE D'AROLLA   3796m.

A beautiful mtn. overlooking the Arolla valley. Undoubtedly the finest and most popular ski peak in the Western Pennine Alps with routes from three huts. Interesting and varied skiing. Flights from Sion can land skiers on the saddle just below the summit. Parties traversing the classic HLR from W to E often make the ascent for its own sake from the Vignettes hut by the E flank.

42   From the Vignettes hut go down to the Col des Vignettes, cross the glacier terrace briefly S below large crevasses and then bear R(W) up the steep E slopes of the mtn. which ease off above c.3350m. (In unfavourable conditions descend SW from the shoulder at the S end of the terrace and immediately head NW up the next glacier branch to join the direct approach at c.3400m.). Continue up broad slopes to the saddle between pt.3772m. and the summit. Reach the top on ski (2-3 h.).

From the Dix hut see Route 32.

From the Chanrion hut see Route 19. In descent the Portons variant sometimes gives better skiing on slopes less exposed to the sun. It avoids the lower part of the Breney glacier by a complex line on the N side of the Portons ridge and should not be attempted in doubtful visibility.

GELÉ - SINGLA - BRULÉ CHAIN

On the frontier ridge, between Mont Vélan and La Singla, only the two summits on either side of the Fenêtre de Durand are ever visited by ski mountaineers based at the Chanrion hut. From the Swiss side of the pass *Mont Avril* (3346m.) is approached by its E flank, finishing on the SE ridge (4-4½ h.). A complex roundabout route to *Mont Gelé* (3518m.) leads from the Swiss Crête Sèche glacier across gaps immediately NW below pt.3061m. and at pt.3144m. (Col du Mont Gelé) so that the summit is reached from the S by the Italian Mont Gelé glacier (5-6 h.). It is possible to complete a most unusual traverse and round trip by skiing S in descent below the Morion chain towards the foot of Mont Clapier, then down W to the Acqua Bianca stream, returning across the Fenêtre de Durand.

From the Col de l'Evêque (Route 20) the E top of the *Pointes d'Oren* (3525m.) can be reached in ½ h. by the pleasant snow crest of its NE ridge.

An ascent of *Mont Brulé* (3591m.) by its long W ridge from the Col Collon (Route 20) makes a splendid ski mountaineering expedition that is seldom undertaken due to the remote position of the mtn. at the head of the Upper Arolla glacier. In good snow conditions skis can be used on the lower part of the ridge (3 h. from Bouquetins biv.). Parties not following the HLR to Zermatt can ski N from the Col Collon down the Upper and Lower Arolla glaciers directly to the valley. The Italian approach to the Col Collon is very seriously exposed to avalanches on the way up to the Principessa di Piemonte hut (2818m.) from where the col is reached in 1 h.

AROLLA WEST

Although the Aigs. Rouges are inaccessible to the ski mountaineer, there remain a few minor tours on the W side of the valley that give pleasant skiing. The unwardened Aigs. Rouges (Waldkirch) hut is reached most safely from La Gouille as the Arolla approach crosses some avalanche prone zones; in either case, contrary to summer practice, it is necessary to ascend higher than the hut, sited on top of a rock barrier, before slanting down to it. It serves as the starting-point for the *Mont de l'Etoile* (3369m.) to the N and the *Pointe de Vouasson* (3489m.)

to the NW, two easy and short outings (2 h.). From the latter summit the ski descent of the N facing Vouasson glacier to Evolène rates as an outstanding ski run subject to safe snow conditions. To the SW of the hut the Col des Ignes (3181m.) provides a connecting passage with the Dix hut (3½ h.), but particular care must be exercised on the steep W flank of the Monts Rouges which is traversed downwards to the Cheilon glacier.

La Roussette (3262m.) makes a pleasant day tour from Arolla and is easily climbed by its S slopes up the Fontanesses cwm from the top station of the Fontanesses ski lift in 2½ h. (see Route 7). The direct descent immediately to the N of Mont Dolin often gives better skiing on slopes less exposed to the sun. Either way complete the run on marked pistes.

L'EVÊQUE   3716m.

An elegant peak that offers an interesting and serious ski route by its N flank with a steep finish. It is approached by heading SE from the Mont Collon glacier plateau (thus far by Route 20) up its small crevassed E branch to the saddle (3528m.) between the Mitre de l'Évêque and l'Évêque. Skis should generally be left here as the slope above tends to form slab avalanches at times. Climb steeply near the L(E) edge of the slope to a slight terrace and continue upwards to join the NW or NE ridge near the top (3½ h. from the Vignettes hut).

AROLLA EAST

The E side of the Arolla valley is flanked by a chain of rock peaks that at first appear to offer the skier no scope. However, there exist a few circuitous tours via the Bertol hut (Route 9) that end with short rock scrambles and therefore appeal to mountaineers in late spring. From the hut skis are merely the best means of reaching these peaks.

For the *Dent de Tsalion* (3589m.), *Aig. de la Tsa* (3668m.) and *Pointes des Douves Blanches* (3664m.) the same approach is taken NE over the upper snowfields of the Mont Miné glacier, crossing a gap on the E ridge of the Pointe de Bertol (3499m.) between its top and pt.3372m., before heading NNW to the E foot of each summit. If the rock is dry, the 80m. E flank of the

pinnacled Aig. de la Tsa gives an attractive little climb on sound
rock by a rising traverse L, with a slab pitch, to a corner and
then three chimneys, II+. Otherwise reach the highest top of
the Pointes des Douves Blanches by its broken E flank, or the
Dent de Tsalion by a few rocks from the SE (2½-3 h. to a summit).
In descent note the possibility of a fine ski run directly to the
valley from the Col de la Tsa.

For the *Dents de Bertol* start towards the Col des Bouquetins
as by Route 34 and reach the saddle between the two summits
by its E slope. A straightforward snow ridge leads to the S peak
(3524m.), while the harder N peak (3547m.) involves a stiff
scramble by the ridge or the gully on its L (about 2 h.).

TÊTE BLANCHE   3724m.

An ideal ski peak that is frequently ascended in conjunction
with the HLR. Most easily climbed from the Bertol hut by its
gentle WNW snow slopes: see Route 34 (2½-3 h.). The more
complex E side approach from the Schönbiel hut by the crevassed
Stockji and Tiefmatten glaciers rates as a fine expedition: reverse
Routes 20 and 34 (5-5½ h.). Allow ¾ h. for the roundabout detour
to the summit from the Col de Valpelline: see Route 20 (6-6½ h.
from the Vignettes hut).

TÊTE DE VALPELLINE   3802m.

A large snow cap rising S of the Col de Valpelline. Slightly less
popular than the Tête Blanche but an equally splendid viewpoint,
especially of the Dent d'Hérens and the Matterhorn. In skiing
terms this summit makes a more worthwhile addition for parties
following the classic HLR from the Vignettes hut to Zermatt:
see Route 20. About ¾ h. from the Col de Valpelline.

DENT D'HÉRENS   4171m.

In late spring competent ski mountaineers can attempt this
difficult mtn. from the Italian Aosta hut by the Grandes Murailles
glacier, SW flank and upper part of the W ridge (5-7 h.). Access
to the unwardened Aosta hut, by descending from the Col de
Valpelline via the Col de la Division, is sometimes seriously
threatened by avalanches (which on several occasions in the
past have badly damaged the building).

VAL D'ANNIVIERS

This valley, S of Sierre, divides at Vissoie. From Grimentz in the W branch access to the Moiry hut (2825m.) in late spring lies via the R(E) shore of the lake and the L(W) bank of the glacier which is crossed E at c.2700m. Several of the minor summits enclosing the Moiry glacier give pleasant ski tours, the *Pointe de Bricola* (3657m.) and the *Pigne de la Lé* (3396m.) being the most popular.

At the roadhead of the main E branch valley Zinal serves as the starting-point for two huts. For the Mountet hut (2886m.), to the S, keep near the valley bed and go straight up the centre of the Zinal glacier, trending towards the R bank higher up. Although the major mtns. surrounding the hut are inaccessible, interesting ski tours lead to the *Trifthorn* (3728m.), *Mont Durand* (3712m.) and the *Pointe de Zinal* (3791m.). The connection with the Schönbiel hut, by the summer route via the Col Durand, is generally too dangerous on the S side to be recommended during the skiing season.

The Tracuit hut (3256m.) is approached on ski by starting S as for the Mountet hut to pt.1906m., then slanting N to the Roc de la Vache and NE to the Col de Tracuit. From here the ascent of the *Bishorn* (4159m.) by the Turtmann glacier gives a splendid ski tour with an extensive panorama from the top as well as a superb close-up view of the Weisshorn. To the NE a complex ski descent to the Turtmann hut and valley is possible.

The three self-contained ski touring areas, detailed briefly above, have no practical links with the HLR.

ZERMATT NORTH-WEST

The Trift side valley is the sole area in the vicinity that as yet remains untouched by mechanized transport systems, though a project has been discussed for the Mettelhorn that would open up fine skiing slopes in the Trift cwm but normally require a return to the valley by cableway lower down. Until late spring the approach to the Rothorn hut is usually exposed to an appreciable avalanche risk, especially below the closed Trift hotel. Ski tourers rarely visit the area and only two relatively minor mtns., the *Wellenkuppe* (3903m.) and the *Äschhorn* (Ober

3669m., Unter 3619m.), can be climbed on ski up to their summit ridges which give easy rock climbs when clear of snow.

BREITHORN   4165m.

Generally considered the easiest 4000m. peak in the Alps, though several others are no harder. The proliferation of uphill transport systems on the approaches to this mtn. has removed some of its attraction for the ski mountaineer, yet at the same time greatly increased its popularity amongst casual day tourers from late February onwards. Thus from Zermatt, starting out from the new Klein Matterhorn cableway terminus (3820m.) reduces the expedition in good conditions to 1½ h. of simple work on ski or foot.

Above the Testa Grigia the ski tows towards the Gobba di Rollin operate in summer only.

In poor visibility orientation without a compass on the Breithorn plateau presents a major problem. An outstanding summit view, especially along the frontier ridge to the Monte Rosa.

43   Take Route 35 to the Breithornpass (2-2½ h. from the Theodulpass, 30 min. from the Klein Matterhorn). Shortly before reaching the pass bear L(NNE) directly towards the summit. Normally leave skis at the foot of the final steep slope immediately below the bergschrund (c.3990m.). Trend slightly L to reach the broad summit ridge a little W of the top (1 h., 3-3½ h. altogether). In the event of icy conditions on the normal route, climb the final slope from L to R up to the E ridge half-way between the gap at pt.4081m. and the top, then follow the narrow crest.

N.B. From the Breithorn plateau both the *Klein Matterhorn* (3883m.) and the *Gobba di Rollin* (3902m.) merely involve short detours and only rate as peak bagging exercises. At the E limit of the Breithorn massif the little known *Roccia Nera* (4075m.) can be climbed on foot in 1¼ h. from the Cesare e Giorgio biv. hut by its steep glacier spur to the corniced frontier ridge, finally moving R along the narrow crest to the top—see also Route 35 N.B.2.

Descent. Almost 20 km. and 2400m. vertical interval of skiing down to Zermatt. Marked pistes give a choice of easy ski runs below the Theodulpass, on the N side, to Schwarzsee (2582m.) or Furgg (2434m.). Weak skiers should avoid the difficult run from Furgg to Furi and instead use the easier Weisse Perle run from Schwarzsee, reached directly over the Upper Theodul and Furgg glaciers or by taking the cable car link from Furgg to Schwarzsee. When sufficient snow extends down to Furi there is also the option of a fine off-piste ski run (beware of crevasses) by the Lower Theodul and Gorner (Boden) glaciers (icy in a dry season).

POLLUX 4091m.

A remote peak of interest to the experienced ski mountaineer and a feasible day tour despite its position. Due to the deteriorating state of the Schwärze glacier and the mechanical transport available to the Theodulpass and Kl. Matterhorn, the normal ski approach to the Schwarztor and to this mtn. now lies across the Breithornpass as by Route 35 (3-4 h.). From the Monte Rosa hut reverse Route 36 (5-5½ h.). In good snow conditions climb the steep W flank, well R of the rock overhang above the Schwarztor, and near its top trend R to join the terminal snow arête of the SW ridge. In icy conditions avoid the flank and climb the entire SW ridge, with fixed wires (not kept in repair) on the short steep riser immediately below the snow arête (1-2 h.). On the return journey beware of longitudinal crevasses on the Grande Verra glacier.

CASTOR 4226m.

An attractive snow mtn. with complex glacier approaches. In terms of the HLR a splendid traverse as well as a peak visited for its own sake. The W side route from the Theodulpass and the normal descent to the Felikjoch are detailed under Route 35 (5-6½ h. to the top). The Zwillings glacier approach from the Monte Rosa hut, described below, varies in difficulty according to the state of the crevasses and may be straightforward with a large track during fine weather.

44   From the Monte Rosa hut slant SW across the Grenz glacier to its junction with the Zwillings glacier between the Schalbetterfluh ridge on the R(W) and pt.3087m. on the L(SE). Work through the lower icefall in roughly the same direction to reach a plateau at c.3140m. and ascend S by the glacier's E branch, keeping near the central barrier that separates the two branches. The slopes are cut by large crevasses which sometimes enforce detours. Above 3500m. avoid more large crevasses by moving L towards the W face of the Liskamm where the route is threatened by avalanches. Trend back to the R(SW) and away from the face to reach the upper plateau by pt.3807m. Beyond, head S up a crevassed cwm that levels out below the Felikjoch (4061m.) ($4\frac{1}{2}$-$5\frac{1}{2}$ h.).

Climb the SE snow ridge on foot without difficulty to the summit (1-$1\frac{1}{2}$ h., $5\frac{1}{2}$-7 h. from the hut).

LISKAMM   W 4480m.   E 4527m.
A massive mtn. overlooking the Grenz glacier; a long narrow ridge connects the two summits and its delicate traverse is normally the preserve of the summer alpinist.

From Felikjoch (see Route 44) the lower W peak is sometimes combined with Castor and in fact gives a longer ski run. From the pass continue NE on ski up the gentle slopes of a broad spur almost to the snow dome marked pt.4214m. Complete the ascent on foot by the SW ridge, with some narrow sections and keeping L of the crest at times (2-$2\frac{1}{2}$ h., $6\frac{1}{2}$-8 h. altogether).

The higher E peak forms a far more serious proposition by its E ridge from the Lisjoch which is reached circuitously from the Monte Rosa hut by leaving Route 45 at c.4180m. to cross the shoulder pt.4260m. ($5\frac{1}{2}$-6 h., direct access from the Gnifetti hut in 2 h.). A delicate climb by the exposed ridge leads to the summit. Constant care must be taken on account of dangerous cornices which tend to be larger and more unstable in spring than in summer; the biggest ones generally build up L of the crest on the undulating section over pt.4343m. and should be turned R on the steep N flank ($2\frac{1}{2}$-3 h., 8-9 h. from the Monte Rosa hut, $4\frac{1}{2}$-5 h. from the Gnifetti hut).

MONTE ROSA

Collectively this group forms the highest massif in the Alps with the greatest conglomeration of 4000m. peaks, all accessible to the ski mountaineer from the Monte Rosa and Gnifetti huts.

Ascents of the Dufourspitze and the Signalkuppe constitute two of the most important Alpine ski tours. Whereas previous dry weather improves the state of the ridge section on the Dufourspitze, consolidated snowfalls create optimum conditions for the badly crevassed Grenz glacier route to the Signalkuppe. Detours from the latter approach (Route 45) enable other summits to be taken in without difficulty; the *Zumsteinspitze* (4563m.) is climbed by its S slope, finishing on a few rocks, in ½ h. from the cwm leading up to the Colle Gnifetti. For the *Parrotspitze* (4436m.), *Ludwigshöhe* (4341m.) and the *Corno Nero* (4321m.) leave the upper plateau of the Grenz glacier around 4200m. according to the line preferred: go up the first two by either of their ridges and the last named by its very short but steep W flank.

The easy N slope of the *Piramide Vincent* (4215m.) first involves a descent on the Italian flank and is most conveniently reached from the Gnifetti hut. At the S limit of the massif the *Punta Giordani* (4046m.), a mere shoulder, nevertheless gives an impressive ski run (crevasse zones) by the Indren glacier on its SW slopes and makes an interesting outing from the Punta Indren cableway terminus (3260m.), sited on its S ridge.

A night at the Gnifetti hut or the Margherita hut enables all these minor summits to be combined without undue effort.

SIGNALKUPPE (PUNTA GNIFETTI) 4556m.

The Margherita hut is situated on the summit. A rewarding but complex glacier expedition, not to be underestimated. The exact line of the route varies from year to year according to the state of the crevasses.

45 From the Monte Rosa hut head SE, keeping L(E) of the Grenz glacier moraine crest, towards the Ober Plattje and trend slightly R past pt.3107m. on to the glacier. In good conditions it is quickest to follow the R bank. Pass a side branch of the glacier, then climb the slope between the rocks rising above pt.3481m. and the icefall to reach a large plateau immediately beyond pt.3696m. which is usually turned on the L. It is, however, often easier to ascend R(W) of the icefall so as to rejoin the above approach on the large plateau. Now either climb the snow cwm on the L of the next icefall or turn it R by broader slopes sometimes exposed to avalanches from the NE face of the Liskamm. Cross a small plateau and continue up the centre of the glacier to the upper plateau around 4200m.

N.B. From the Gnifetti hut this point is reached by going up the E bank of the Lis glacier to the shoulder (4246m.) immediately R of pt.4260m. and then traversing NE slightly downwards below the W ridge of the Parrotspitze.

Soon trend L(NNE) into the open cwm that leads up to the Colle Gnifetti at its head between the Zumsteinspitze and the Signalkuppe. Pass L of an ice barrier at c.4400m. and above bear R(SE) directly towards the summit. Climb the final steep slope, with a few loose rocks, on foot to the top and the Margherita hut (6-8 h. from the Monte Rosa hut, 3½-4 h. from the Gnifetti hut).

DUFOURSPITZE   4634m.
The highest peak in Switzerland and second highest in the Alps. In fresh snow the W ridge becomes strenuous and tiring. Icy conditions or a strong wind make the climbing on the summit rock crest delicate. No real crevasse problems compared with the Signalkuppe and Castor.

First ascent: J. Birkbeck, C. Hudson, C. & J. G. Smyth and E. J. Stephenson with U. Lauener, J. and M. Zumtaugwald, 1 August 1855. First winter ascent: C., E., G. and V. Sella (brothers) with D. and J. P. Maquignaz, 19 February 1889. First ski ascent: H. Moser and O. Schuster, 1898.

46   From the Monte Rosa hut ascend SE, keeping L(E) of the Grenz glacier moraine crest, towards the Ober Plattje. At c.3000m., below the top of the moraine, bear slightly L up the centre of a steep slope which is bounded by two rock arms (pt.3303m. and pt.3277m. on the Ober Plattje) where it meets the Monte Rosa glacier. Head ESE up its L(W) side, soon crossing a crevasse zone around 3400m. Move L of an ice barrier on this long escarpment above the Grenz glacier and go up two successive glacier cwms, passing R of pt.3823m. At c.4000m. slant R up the open slopes known as the Satteldohle (named on LK 25) towards the Sattel (4359m., badly placed spot height on LK 50). Leave skis at about 4300m. below the bergschrund. Now go up a steep slope to join the W ridge just L of the Sattel (5-6 h.).

Follow the snow/ice crest and then traverse a rock hump to a gap. Climb the broad snow ridge which narrows and eases off to the final rock section. Reach the summit by a short chimney ($1\frac{1}{2}$-3 h., $6\frac{1}{2}$-9 h. from the hut).

NORDEND 4609m.
Recommended for the splendid ski run from the Silbersattel which surpasses the Dufourspitze descent provided that the icefall below the saddle is well snowed up. As by Route 46 to around 4000m. Climb the ruptured glacier basin between the Nordend and the Dufourspitze to the Silbersattel (4517m.), turning most of the huge crevasses on the L. A line to the R nearer the Dufourspitze, as shown on the LK 50 ski map, is nowadays usually impracticable. Climb to the top by the narrow S ridge with large cornices on the R, finishing on a few rocks ($6\frac{1}{2}$-9 h.).

JÄGERHORN 3969m.
FILLARHÖRNER Kl.3620m. Gr.3678m.
Sometimes climbed as training tours from the Monte Rosa hut. Approach by Route 23. For the Jägerhorn ascend the steep glacier cwm (bergschrund) to the Jägerjoch and scramble up rocks past the Gallarate biv. hut to the fore peak; the short but hard traverse to the proper summit is rarely made. The Fillarhörner are reached easily by the upper slopes of the Gorner glacier. The shortest access to these tops in fact starts from the Stockhorn cableway terminus: see Route 24.

CIMA DI JAZZI 3804m.
An easy summit with an outstanding view of the Monte Rosa E face that is nevertheless not as dramatic as the close-up prospect from the Jägerhorn. Due to the availability of uphill transport

that has transformed this tour into a short outing the mtn. is climbed by large numbers of skiers, often improperly equipped for a glacier tour, as a prelude to the long run down the Findeln glacier in spring.

47   Reach the Stockhornpass (3394m., variable on LK 50) from Zermatt by Route 24 (1 h. from the cableway terminus) or from the Monte Rosa hut by Route 23 (3-3½ h.). Ascend a broad, gentle glacier spur (really the continuation of the Stockhorn ridge that divides the Findeln and Gorner glaciers) towards pt.3636m. (Torre di Castelfranco on LK 25). Coming from the Monte Rosa hut this spur can be joined straight from the Gorner glacier by continuing E below the Stockhornpass. Leave it at c.3500m. and traverse a shallow cwm up to the equally broad but steeper NW spur of the Cima di Jazzi which leads to the top (1½ h., 2½ h. from the cableway terminus, 4½-5 h. from the Monte Rosa hut). Variations possible, normally well tracked.

Descent. While one can return to the cableway terminus or to the Monte Rosa hut, and also continue to the Britannia hut (Route 23) or to Saas Almagell (Route 37), by far the most rewarding ski run lies down the Findeln glacier, taking its L bank near the tongue so as to later join the marked piste near Grünsee. This run gives 2200m. downhill skiing to Zermatt. When the snow line has risen above the valley floor, board the gondola cableway at Gant or the chair lift at Findeln accordingly.

STRAHLHORN   4190m.
A relatively easy 4000m. peak. Frequently combined with the HLR traverse from the Monte Rosa hut or Zermatt to the Britannia hut (Routes 23-25). Often climbed for its own sake from the latter hut and in any case visited much more in spring than in summer when troublesome crevasses open up on the W side approach.

48   From the Britannia hut ski SW down a short steep slope, losing 50m., and cross the Hohlaub glacier horizontally to pass immediately E of the rock islet pt.3143m. Ascend the L(W)

bank of the Allalin glacier and beyond the side branch rising W
to the Allalinpass bear L of a crevasse zone at c.3350m. before
moving back above towards the Rimpfischhorn E face. Continue
SSW up to the Adlerpass (3802m.) (3½ h.).

Reach the Adlerpass by Route 23 from the Monte Rosa hut
(6-6½ h.) and by Route 24 or 25 from Zermatt (4-5 h.).

In suitable snow conditions now traverse briefly E into a
steep glacier cwm, sometimes cut by a large crevasse, and climb
it on ski to reach the upper NW slopes on the L(E) of the small
shoulder marked pt.3917m. Otherwise, from the Adlerpass
climb the snow ridge (icy bits possible) on foot to this shoulder.
N.B. Coming from the Britannia hut one can head S straight up
the cwm without going to the Adlerpass. Now continue easily
ESE, leaving the fore peak pt.4127m. to the R, to a few rocks
at the summit (1½ h., 5 h. from the Britannia hut, 7½-8 h. from
the Monte Rosa hut, 5½-6½ h. from Zermatt).

FLUCHTHORN   3790m.

A minor snow peak that makes a pleasant training tour from
the Britannia hut, also suitable when the weather puts the
higher mtns. in the vicinity out of condition. Climbed by its
N slopes, passing W of the rock islet pt.3443m. in the centre of
the Allalin glacier, to reach the summit dome from the W
(3-3½ h.).

RIMPFISCHHORN   4198m.

Harder than the other 4000m. peaks hereabouts with a short
rock climb (II in dry conditions) at the finish. The glacier
shoulder by pt.4009m. at the WSW foot of the summit rocks is
reached from the Britannia hut by crossing the Allalinpass (see
Route 48) to the Mellich glacier before making a rising traverse
on the W side of the mtn., passing immediately below two
obvious ribs marked pt.3556m. and pt.3655m. This shoulder
can also be approached from Blauherd (Zermatt) by the normal
Fluhalp summer route via the Pfulwe and the long S spur of
the Längfluh glacier, finally on foot. (The Fluhalp hotel is
occasionally open in spring.) Leave skis here and start up a
broad snow gully between the twin towers above, then slant L
on to the rock spur of the fore peak below half height, climb its

sound rocks and continue L along the narrow mixed crest to
the nearby main top (5½-6 h.). N.B. From the Täsch hut the
above route can be joined near the Allalinpass by traversing
below the SW flank of the Feekopf. In descent a fine run down
the centre of the Mellich glacier leads directly to the Täschalp.

ALLALINHORN   4027m.

Undoubtedly the most popular ski peak in the vicinity of Saas
Fee and most often climbed as a day tour by using the Längfluh
cableway. Skis can sometimes be used almost to the top, but
are normally left at the Feejoch.

49   From the Längfluh inn head S up the gently inclined Fee
glacier and keep well L of the séracs around the rock islet
pt.3173m.

From the Britannia hut join this approach at c.3150m. on a
plateau by following Route 38.

Continue S up the centre of the broad glacier cwm, bounded
to the L(E) by the NE ridge of the Allalinhorn and to the R(W)
by the rock barrier falling NNE from the Feekopf. At c.3200m.
trend L to avoid crevasses and above return to the R. Higher
up, a steeper slope is usually split by large crevasses and the best
line varies according to the state of the glacier. The slope then
eases off to the Feejoch (c.3810m.) below and W of the summit
cone.

Climb steep snow to a slight shoulder and slant R before
going up to the summit ridge R(SE) of the nearby top (¾ h. from
the Feejoch, 4½ h. from the Längfluh inn, 5-5½ h. from the
Britannia hut).

Descent. For the easiest run to Saas Fee, at c.3150m. bear R
above the icefall and ski down N of pt.3081m. to join the
Felskinn piste (Route 26). The direct piste from the Längfluh
cableway terminus gives a steep run with several alternatives
below the intermediate station at Spielboden (2452m.).

FEEKOPF   3888m.

An unimportant summit that is reached very easily via the
Alphubeljoch from the gentle upper slopes of the central branch
of the Fee glacier; see Route 50. Fine skiing. The proposed

cableway extension from Felskinn via an intermediate station at c.3500m. on the NE ridge of the Allalinhorn to this peak has for the time being been rejected by the Swiss government. Its construction would disfigure the immediate surroundings and enable the Alphubel approach to be joined at 3750m. by a mere 10 min. of downhill skiing.

ALPHUBEL   4206m.

The normal ski route takes the broken glacier slopes covering the E flank of this distinctive mtn. which is capped by a long summit plateau. Mist makes it virtually impossible to determine the highest point. More complex crevasse work than on the Allalinhorn. In perfect conditions the top can be reached on ski, otherwise climb the summit cwm above the bergschrund on foot.

50   (a)   From the Längfluh inn start SSW up the central branch of the Fee glacier towards the Alphubeljoch. At first keep nearer the Feekopf spur, but soon bear SW up the R-hand (W) terrace of this glacier branch. Above c.3250m. this terrace develops into a narrow raised band which is cut by numerous crevasses. Ascend steeply S and exit on to broad gentle slopes at c.3600m.

   (b)   From the Britannia hut follow Route 38 to c.3100m. on the broad glacier cwm to the N of the Feejoch. Cross it W and enter the lower (E) band of the central branch of the Fee glacier by passing above and S of the rock islet pt.3173m. via a gap near the foot of the NNE spur of the Feekopf. This band is separated from the upper one by an ice barrier. Ascend S, parallel to the Längfluh approach, and around 3500m. work through a badly ruptured section to the easy slopes above. Trend R(SW) to join (a) at c.3650m.

   Now bear W up straightforward slopes, gradually veering further R to arrive due E of the top at c.3950m. below the final riser. Cross a bergschrund and climb a steep cwm to the summit plateau (5 h. from the Längfluh inn, 5½-6 h. from the Britannia hut). (The upper part of this ascent can be reached from the Täsch hut by crossing the Alphubeljoch, 5½ h. to the top.)

   Descent.   To link up with the easier Felskinn piste (Route 26) reverse the Britannia hut approach to the flat glacier basin below the cableway terminus. The direct piste from the Längfluh cableway terminus gives a steep run with several alternatives below the intermediate station at Spielboden (2452m.).

MISCHABEL GROUP
Defined here as the mtns. between the Mischabeljoch and the Riedpass. Not a region for skiers. When the Dom hut path has cleared of snow (late May/early June), mountaineers prepared to carry their skis thus far can climb the *Dom* (4545m.) via the Festijoch and its N flank, an expedition first carried out on ski by Arnold Lunn (Britain's only pioneer of ski mountaineering) with Joseph Knubel in June 1917. On the N side of the chain a ski approach to the *Nadelhorn* (4327m.) leads from the Bordier hut up the Ried glacier via the *Ulrichshorn* (3925m.) or directly to the Windjoch and the NE ridge which gives some rock scrambling. Access to the Bordier hut from Grächen requires stable snow conditions.

WEISSMIES GROUP
The cableway from Saas Grund to the Triftalp (2283m.) has shortened the approach to the Weissmies hut (2726m.), the best base for a ski ascent of the *Weissmies* (4023m.) by the Hohlaub and Trift glaciers to the SW ridge. The other ski route from Saas Almagell via new Almagell hut (2860m.) under the Dri Horlini to the Zwischbergenpass and the SSE ridge is equally an attractive proposition. An ascent of the *Fletschhorn* (3996m.) by the glacier branch enclosed between the Jägigrat and the SW ridge of the Lagginhorn has become difficult, dangerous and consequently impractical in recent years due to the deteriorating state of the icefall. An approach to this mtn. from Simplon village by the Griessernen glacier and the Rossboden glacier, best reached via the gap at pt.3012m. rather than the harder direct route shown on the LK 50 ski map, to join the NE ridge (easy broken rocks) at an unmistakable snow shoulder is a serious and strenuous undertaking.

INDEX

133

135

H L R in summer

An easy mountaineering tour with noticeable differences
in the route line followed, especially over glaciers. Gr:
F+/PD- in good conditions. Rope, axe and crampons
essential. Spare slings useful. The route is normally
too serious for mountain walkers and scramblers unless
accompanied by an experienced alpinist. Facilities at
huts are generally much better in summer, and more
convenient access to provisioning at villages often means
that pack loads can be reduced compared with the ski
touring period. Followers of the summer route are
advised to consult also the corresponding ski sections
with regard to comments about route finding, visability
problems and landmarks.

Argentière - Argentière Hut
From the S-bend bridge over the Arve river on the main
road below Argentière follow a minor road on E side of
river to Grands Montets cableway station. Take a wide
path cutting steeply through the wooded slopes above the
R side of the Argentière gl. valley, to a point where it
bends R(SW) and leads gradually towards the Croix de
Lognan cableway station further up. At this pt. (1752m.)
take on the L a much smaller and steeper track which
zigzags up to the Chalet Militaire de Lognan (2032m.), $1\frac{1}{2}$h.

Above this the path reaches the moraine crest on the R
side of the gl. and follows it to above the icefall. Now
descend to the gl. and follow the R side to the Moraine
des Rognons. Generally when there is plenty of snow
(i.e. winter) it is quicker to remain on the gl. below the
Moraine. The path however crosses these rocks by slabs

and little streams to a platform at the SE end from where it is possible to descend to the gl. over large blocks(2 h.).

Continue up the R side of the gl. below the Aig. Verte and Les Droites, to about 2700m. Now cross the gl. to the opposite side and reach a moraine which is not evident from afar. Cross the moraine and slant up to the E to reach a good track on the lateral moraine leading directly to hut (1 h., $4\frac{1}{2}$-5 h.). Where rocks are evident the route is indicated by red paint flashes.

Cableway shortcut from Plan/Croix de Lognan. From this station (1975m.) follow the obvious large track E to join the regular path not far above the Chalet Militaire. Saves $1\frac{1}{4}$h.

Cableway shortcut from the Grands Montets top station (3297m.). Commonly practised by climbers with big loads. Descend rocky path to the Col des Grands Montets(3233m.) in a few min. Now descend the Rognons gl. towards the NE, generally with a short steep section at the start followed by gentler slopes with a few crevasses. Pass just L of a small rognon (3000m.) and continue down almost to the top of the Moraine des Rognons before turning to the SE and crossing the S branch of the Rognons gl. to reach the R side of the Argentière gl. ($1\frac{1}{2}$h.). Now continue as for the last part of the regular walking route (1 h., $2\frac{1}{2}$ h. from cableway station).

Argentière Hut-Trient Hut

From the hut follow a path W down the R side of the main gl. until reaching moraine and loose rocks that form the R side of the Chardonnet gl. Go up these and get on to the badly crevassed gl. Work up carefully bearing L to the branch leading to the Chardonnet col. The upper slopes are straightforward and much less steep. Cross a small bergschrund and climb some easy rocks to the pass (2¾ h.).

It is far easier to ascend the L side of the gl. from its base, all the way to the col. This is longer but more comfortable. Go further down and get on to the L side moraine of the Chardonnet gl. by a small track to follow the moraine crest until it is convenient to slant R on to the gl. at 2850m. Continue straight up, shortly joining the more direct route, to the col, 3323m. (3¼ h.).

On the other side a steep snow slope (crampons) drops 60m. to a sometimes large bergschrund. According to conditions, either descend direct, or slant L (facing out) to rock which can be followed down in steps with two cracks to rejoin the slope not far above the bergschrund. Normally the latter can be jumped, taking the usual precautions. Abseil flakes and old slings on the rocks need careful examination.

Now descend the upper slope of the Saleina gl. for 200m, then traverse NE over snow and moraine under the Gde. Fourche into the gl. bay beyond and below the Fenêtre de Saleinaz. A snow and rock slope leads with some steepness at the top to this col, 3267m. (1¾ h.). Now go due N across the Trient gl. plateau, shortly tracking NE to cross Col d'Orny (3098m.) where a large track leads in a few min. to the Trient hut (1 h., 5½-6 h.).

Trient Hut - Champex

Leaving the Trient hut, follow edge of the gl. plateau W then N for 15 min., and near the top of the Trient icefall cross the small snow and rock W spur of the Petite Pte. d'Orny to continue immediately across a steeper slope into the ridge gap almost due N; the Fenêtre des Chamois

(2985m.), not marked on map. Go through first gap on R and descend the N side gully, steep snow or rubble, or use rocks on L side. Continue down rough boulder slopes and scree ENE in the Combe des Ecandies to a small hollow at pt. 2364m. where an improving track is found. Follow this down the bed of the Arpette valley, keeping R at the Arpette chalet, to join after a short wooded zone the small road (1498m.) running SE to Champex village (1477m.) (3 h.).

Champex - Bourg St. Pierre
As for the ski tour, go round by road (bus service) via Orsières.

Recommended Variation. More correct summer HLR.
Argentière Hut - La Fouly - Bourg St. Pierre

Under the E side of the Col du Chardonnet proceed down the R side of the Saleina gl. as for the ski tour Route 28, and cross the Planereuses, Upper Crête Sèche and the subsequent cols to the A Neuve hut (8 h. from Argentière hut). Compared with the skiing conditions described in Route 28, summer conditions will reveal open crevasse zones on all gl. sections, and the gullies ascended and descended over the 3 cols will be dry and gritty, possibly with icy patches.

From the A Neuve hut descend the clearly waymarked valley path, S at first and steep with a fixed chain section, then SE to the A Neuve chalets (1593m.) and La Fouly hamlet. Chalet bunkhouse accommodation (2 h.). Alternative accommodation at Ferret hamlet (1700m.) further up the road.

Ferret to Bourg St. Pierre, over the Col (Sud) des Planards (2732m.). Follow jeep road SE up L side of

valley to Les Ars-Dessus (1955m.), chalets on a path
above and E of the valley one. From here follow a steep
zigzag track E up the L side of the Vaylat stream to a
stony section trending L to a ruined chalet (2373m.).
From here follow a discontinuous track E for a short way
to where it soon turns N. Continue N for a short way,
then circle round and upwards to the R (SE) to cross the
shoulder behind (N of) the Clocher de l'Arpalle (2617m.)
and enter the Arpalle cwm. Directly ahead, slant up a
steep rubble slope to the Planards col ($3\frac{3}{4}$-$4\frac{1}{4}$ h. from
Ferret).

On the other side descend a steep rough hanging slope
almost due N (do not descend due E), soon bearing R
(NE) and coming down to the Gouille du Dragon tarn.
From its outfall (2618m., S side) a vague track can be
picked up in the rocks and followed down in a slanting
line E under pt. 2557m. to join the Planards valley bed
at c. 2250m. The path eventually emerges above the
Toules barrage. Work N above barrage lake to chalets
called La Letta (1907m.). From here descend a zigzag
jeep road NE to the old roadhead under the dam(1730m.),
or go down to the barrage and cross the dam wall to
join the Great St. Bernard road about 3 km. S of Bourg
St. Pierre ($1\frac{3}{4}$ h., $5\frac{1}{2}$-6 h. from Ferret). Bus service
along St. Bernard road.

Bourg St. Pierre - Valsorey Hut
Leave village by a small road on L at top (S) end, which
undercrosses the main St. Bernard road and enters the
Valsorey valley. Follow road to the Cordonna chalets
(1834m.). Continue by a mule path with a very gradual
ascent. Soon after crossing a prominent stream, reach

a fork, signpost, just below pt. 2152m. Now go L and up to the Amont chalets (2197m.). From here take the lower of two paths which mounts the Six Rodzes rockband above (2352.5m.), latterly up a gully with a cable and ladder at the top, to reach open slopes called the Grands Plans (2501.8m.), below the Meitin cwm. Ascend NE over grass stones and snow patches, path becoming poor, to a low relief rock spur, pt. 2614m. Work L on to this and follow its L side before moving R on to the easy crest, which leads to moraine where the hut is found. It is much further up the spur than appearances suggest from below ($4\frac{1}{2}$-5 h.).

Valsorey Hut - Col du Sonadon - Chanrion Hut

Leave hut following a small cairned track NE over scree and snow to reach the Meitin snowfield at the foot of a rock rib which borders the L(W) side of the couloir coming down from the Col du Meitin. From here slant progressively R(E) and climb fairly steep snow and broken rock (crampons) to a snow saddle which overlooks the large snowfield called the Plateau du Couloir, under the S face of the Combin de Valsorey. The saddle is normally attained some 150-200m. N of pt. 3664m. (at this spot, bivouac shelter). This somewhat higher level is close to foot of the SW rib of the Combin de Valsorey ($2\frac{1}{2}$ h.). Now descend the snow plateau ESE, stonefall possible, and go down a short steep section constricted by the ends of two rockbands, crevassed, bergschrund possible, on to the last snowfield of the Sonadon gl. Cross this in the same direction to a short riser and the Sonadon col (3504m.), 45 min. ($3\frac{1}{4}$ h. from Valsorey hut).

From the col descend snow slopes briefly E to near the base of the Grafeneire SE ridge on your L. Now contour

142

and cross gl. S along a terrace band to small bay on other side under the Col d'Amiante. Descend L(ENE) with crevasses in a hollow to gl. plateau below. Follow this keeping R, under the Tête Blanche, passing just below a rock island near the base of its NE ridge at pt. 3094m. Easy but crevassed slopes, keeping R, come down to a flanking rockband under pt. 2953m. Now a gl. trench under these rocks gives access at 2700m. to a moraine corridor across the rockband, slightly upwards, then horizontally E beside pt. 2697m. to a somewhat higher opening in the ridge beyond at pt. 2735.7m. From here a poor track goes down a slight hollow ENE, soon bearing R (S) to cross a stream, c. 2520m., at the head of the Plan Petit Giètro, where the Fenêtre de Durand path is joined. Either go down this, or steeper but much shorter, from where the former vague track bears R in the slight hollow, continue straight down a well used shortcut, over steep rough grass slopes, both ways joining in the valley bottom at footbridge 2185m. Get on to the jeep road above and follow this for 250m. to a footpath on the L, leading as a shortcut above the road to the road again higher up, then by the road again to a signpost indicating another shortcut due N over the Paume pasture and past the Neuf chalet to the Chanrion hut ($3\frac{1}{2}$-4 h., 7 h. from Valsorey).

Chanrion Hut - Vignettes Hut

There are upper and lower approaches to the Otemma gl. Upper: A vague track mounts E over grass and scree to a small but well defined traverse path. This works SE below a large rockband and over steep grass to reach a promontory (2720m.) overlooking the gl. From here

descend an easy scree couloir facing SSE for some distance, then traverse L on to the gl. at c. 2600m. (1¼ h.).
Lower: Follow a descending path S to jeep road at pt. 2414m. and take this to a bend above chalets at pt. 2337m. Short-cut this loop. Either join the original path in a few min. which rises a little round shoulder 2467m. before descending then traversing to finish on top of a rockface at lower end of the Otemma gl. Or, take jeep road at a lower level, via pt. 2329m. which ends at the base of the rockface, pt. 2357m. Either way, traverse on to the gl., somewhat loose and unpleasant, work into the middle and go up at length and without incident to the low, broad and distinct snow saddle of the Col de Chermotane (3053m.).

From here bear L and cross almost level snow N to a short steep slope rising to a shoulder immediately L of pt. 3162m. Continue horizontally in the same direction across a snow terrace to the Col des Vignettes, then turn R along a track in a rock spine to the Vignettes hut (5-6 h.).

Vignettes Hut - Col de l'Evêque - Bouquetins Hut
Return along path in rock spine W to the Vignettes col. Now cross snow terrace horizontally S and pass R (W) of pt. 3162m. to drop down a short steep slope on to the Col de Chermotane. Work SE over the plateau of the Mont Collon gl., trending R after passing under the N face of the Petit Mt. Collon, and finally climbing always at an easy angle S towards the Ptes. d'Oren on the frontier ridge ahead. More numerous crevasses, with the Col du Petit Mt. Collon on your R. Trend L without incident and reach the broad saddle of the Col de l'Evêque (2¼ h.), 3392m. On the other side go down a snowfield almost due E to the edge of a steeper crevassed zone. Keep R

and join the stony frontier ridge on your R near point
3263. 7m. Follow this ridge down to Col Collon (3087m.).
Now descend on snow due N for 15 min. before bearing
R (E) under the large rock island of La Vierge to reach
in another 15 min. to the NE the moraine corner where
the Bouquetins hut is perched. No warden or provisions
at this small hut ($1\frac{1}{4}$ h., $3\frac{1}{2}$ h. from Vignettes hut).

Bouquetins Hut - Col du Mont Brulé - Col de Valpelline - Schönbiel Hut

From the hut descend S to the gl. and go up the huge bay
SE to the foot of the Brulé col, under and R of the Pte.
de la Gde. Arête (3350. 5m.) further L (N). About 800m.
to the S appears the equally easy looking Col de Tsa de
Tsan which must be ignored. From a small bergschrund
ascend the top slope of the col, often scree, slanting R
to L. The best crossing place is a short distance S of
the lowest pt. (3213m.) of the saddle ($1\frac{1}{4}$ h.). On the
other side, level with the S-most bay of the Haut Tsa
de Tsan gl., descend NW in the middle of the slope and
reach the lower end of the large gl. terrace lying below
the Bouquetins. Contour in a wide arc keeping L (N
then NE) to below the Col des Bouquetins (crevasses)
up to your L. Continue ENE near the centre of the gl.
then trend L up a snow cwm with crevasses towards the
rock wall of the Tête Blanche at the top, below which
the Col de Valpelline (3568m.) is reached by a steeper
slope ($2\frac{1}{2}$ h.).

Descend the Stockji gl. ENE with more numerous,
large and troublesome crevasses needing care, passing
under the Col d'Hérens (L) and keeping somewhat L beyond this before trending R (ESE) to reach on the other

side the haven of the Stockji rock spine at pt. 3041m. A
small track goes E along the spine, then traverses under
R(S) side of pt. 3091.8m., to reach a snow saddle beyond
in a few min. From here descend a large open snow
couloir N, steep and crampons should be worn when bed
is frozen; or in soft snow glissade with care. At the
bottom cross the dry Schönbiel gl. NW to near pt. 2738m.
where the moraine path is joined, leading down SE and
briefly to the Schönbiel hut (2 h., $5\frac{1}{4}$-$5\frac{3}{4}$ h. from Bouquetins hut).

Schönbiel Hut - Zermatt
A well marked trail does down the L side moraines of
the Zmutt gl., across the entrance to the Arben side
valley, then in grassy trenches and past pretty chalets
to Zmutt hamlet before entering patches of woodland
which eventually lead to the metalled road at the main
cableway station outside Zermatt (3 h. or less).

Parties wishing to continue by a choice of glacier cols
to Saas Fee should consult the guidebook Pennine Alps
East. Routes above the Theodul and behind the Klein
Matterhorn, on the Italian side of the Breithorn-Mte.
Rosa chain, are described in Pennine Alps Central.

Variations
Among several, the most common but improper set of
variations is to start at Le Tour above Argentière and
proceed to the Albert Premier hut with part chairlift
assistance if desired. Then by one of the Cols du Tour
to the Trient hut. From here over col d'Orny and down
the valley path to La Breya where a chairlift can be

taken down to Champex. Then missing out the Planards col, by adopting the soft option of going from Champex to Bourg St. Pierre via Orsières by bus. After reaching the Vignettes hut, the valley trail is taken to Arolla, then reascent to the Bertol hut. From here the Col d'Hérens is crossed to the Schönbiel hut and Zermatt.